More Praise for *Kiss That Frog!*

"Brian Tracy gives us a road map of how we can turn negatives into positives and live a healthy, rewarding, and contributing life."
—**Patricia Fripp, Past President, National Speakers Association, and author of *Get What You Want***

"This book shows you how to let go of negatives, find the positive in every situation, and become an optimistic, high-performance person."
—**Jack Canfield, CEO, Jack Canfield Companies**

"Brian Tracy has done it again! *Kiss That Frog!* is a classic about turning negatives into positives. Get ready for a life-changing read."
—**Pat Williams, Senior Vice President, Orlando Magic, and author of *Leadership Excellence***

"This wonderful, uplifting book shows you how to release negatives and become a completely positive person."
—**Harvey Mackay, author of the #1 *New York Times* bestseller *Swim with the Sharks Without Being Eaten Alive***

"If your memories of yesterday are greater than your dreams for tomorrow, read this book and watch your life turn around, and experience more joy and happiness as a result."
—**Todd Duncan, *New York Times* bestselling author of *Time Traps***

"For people who *really* and *truly* want to break free of their limitations and move toward having the life of their dreams, this is the book to read! Both thought provoking and inspiring—you owe it to yourself to read this book and utilize these great teachings!"
—**John Assaraf, bestselling author and entrepreneurial coach**

"Another winner from Brian Tracy! It's a handbook for personal responsibility to achieve success. Read it. Implement what you learn. Have confidence about your future."
—**Bill Bachrach, CSP, CPAE, author of *Values-Based Financial Planning* and coauthor of *High-Trust Leadership***

"Every decade or so, an absolute gem of wisdom appears in print. Brian and Christina have cut and polished a priceless gift offering life-changing principles for success, regardless of the circumstances. They make the profound simple and the impossible doable."
—**Denis Waitley, author of *Seeds of Greatness***

Kiss
That
Frog!

OTHER BOOKS BY BRIAN TRACY

Kiss That Frog!

12 Great Ways to Turn Negatives into Positives in Your Life and Work

Brian Tracy

Christina Tracy Stein

BK

Berrett–Koehler Publishers, Inc.
San Francisco
a BK Life book

Berrett-Koehler Publishers, Inc.
235 Montgomery Street, Suite 650
San Francisco, CA 94104-2916
Tel: (415) 288-0260   Fax: (415) 362-2512   www.bkconnection.com

ORDERING INFORMATION
Quantity sales. Special discounts are available on quantity purchases by corporations, associations, and others. For details, contact the "Special Sales Department" at the Berrett-Koehler address above.
Individual sales. Berrett-Koehler publications are available through most bookstores. They can also be ordered directly from Berrett-Koehler: Tel: (800) 929-2929; Fax: (802) 864-7626; www.bkconnection.com
Orders for college textbook/course adoption use. Please contact Berrett-Koehler: Tel: (800) 929-2929; Fax: (802) 864-7626.
Orders by U.S. trade bookstores and wholesalers. Please contact Ingram Publisher Services, Tel: (800) 509-4887; Fax: (800) 838-1149; E-mail: customer.service@ingram publisherservices.com; or visit www.ingrampublisherservices.com/Ordering for details about electronic ordering.

Berrett-Koehler and the BK logo are registered trademarks of Berrett-Koehler Publishers, Inc.

Printed in the United States of America

Berrett-Koehler books are printed on long-lasting acid-free paper. When it is available, we choose paper that has been manufactured by environmentally responsible processes. These may include using trees grown in sustainable forests, incorporating recycled paper, minimizing chlorine in bleaching, or recycling the energy produced at the paper mill.

Library of Congress Cataloging-in-Publication Data
Tracy, Brian.
Kiss that frog : 12 great ways to turn negatives into positives in your life and work / Brian Tracy and Christina Tracy Stein. —1st ed.
    p. cm.
"A BK Life book."
Includes bibliographical references and index.
ISBN 978-1-60994-280-9 (hbk. : alk. paper)
1. Positive psychology. 2. Positivism. 3. Attitude (Psychology)
4. Success. I. Stein, Christina Tracy. II. Title.
BF204.6.T73 2012
650.1—dc23   2011045852

FIRST EDITION
17 16 15 14 13 12   10 9 8 7 6 5 4 3 2 1

Copyediting: PeopleSpeak
Book design and composition: Beverly Butterfield, Girl of the West Productions
Cover design: Leslie Waltzer
Author photos: Jason Wallis and Mina Neuberg

To my wife, Barbara, the light of my life, and to my wonderful children—Christina, Michael, David, and Catherine—all of whom are living proof of the high self-esteem, high self-confidence adults that people become when they receive an unbroken flow of unconditional love throughout their lives.

BRIAN TRACY

To my husband, Damon, who encourages me with his unconditional love and support, and my three children, Julia, Will, and Scarlett, who make every day an adventure full of lessons, laughter, and love.

CHRISTINA TRACY STEIN

CONTENTS

The Frog and the Princess

You are here on this earth to do something wonderful with your life, to experience happiness and joy, wonderful relationships, excellent health, complete prosperity, and total fulfillment. So, why aren't you living the life of your dreams already?

If you want to know the reasons for your happiness or unhappiness, success or lack of success, wins or losses, look in the nearest mirror. The quality of your thinking about whom you see in the mirror largely determines the quality of your life. If you change your thinking about yourself, you change your life—almost immediately.

There is nothing either good or bad, but thinking makes it so.

WILLIAM SHAKESPEARE

A Fairy Tale

Once upon a time, according to the fairy tale, a handsome prince was turned into an ugly frog by a spiteful witch. Her curse could be broken only if he was kissed by a princess, something the witch was sure would never happen.

Once upon that same time, a beautiful princess longed for a handsome prince she could marry, but he hadn't appeared in her life. One day, while walking alone in the woods by a small lake, she saw an ugly frog who was living in the woods. As the princess sat quietly by the water, thinking about her situation and longing for a handsome prince to come along, the frog hopped up to her and spoke.

He told her that he was actually a handsome prince, and if she would just kiss him, he would turn into the prince that he had been before and he would marry her and love her forever after.

The idea seemed absurd, but with great reluctance, she summoned up her courage and character and kissed the frog right on the lips.

As he had promised, he immediately turned into a handsome prince. He kept his word and married her, and they lived happily ever after.

The Moral of the Story

It seems that almost everyone has a block, or more than one, that holds him or her back from becoming a truly happy, healthy, joyful person, looking forward to each new day with excitement and anticipation.

What is the "frog" in your life that you need to "kiss" before you can achieve all that is possible for you? What are the negative experiences in your life that you need to embrace, deal with, and use to transform yourself into the amazing person you are capable of becoming?

What We All Want

The great aim of human life is to enjoy happiness and peace of mind. Every normal person wants to enjoy and experience the positive emotions of love, pleasure, satisfaction, and fulfillment.

Perhaps the greatest discovery in psychology and individual fulfillment is that the biggest obstacles that stand between you and an extraordinary life are usually negative mental attitudes toward yourself and others. Only when you learn to "kiss that frog," continually making it a habit to seek and find something positive and worthwhile in every person and experience, will you unlock your full potential for success.

In this book, based on five thousand talks and seminars with more than five million people in fifty-eight countries (Brian), and many thousands of hours of work in counseling and psychology (Christina), you will learn a series of simple but powerful methods and techniques that you can use immediately to change from negative thinking to positive thinking and turn every problem in your life into a benefit of some kind. You will learn how to become a completely confident person and release your full potential to live an extraordinary life.

These tools and strategies have worked for millions of people all over the world, and they will work for you. Let's begin.

1

Seven Truths About You

Your natural state is to be happy, peaceful, joyous, and full of excitement at being alive. In this natural state you wake up each morning eager to start the day. You feel wonderful about yourself and your relationships with the people in your life. You enjoy your work and derive a great sense of satisfaction from making a contribution that makes a difference. Your primary goal should be to organize your life in such a way that this is how you feel most of the time.

As a fully functioning, fully mature adult, you should be doing things every day that move you toward the fulfillment of your potential. You should feel grateful for all your blessings in every area. If you are unhappy or dissatisfied in any part of your life, something is not right in your thoughts, feelings, or actions, and it needs to be corrected.

The starting point in unlocking your full potential is to realize that you *already* are a prince or princess, deep down inside.

Most folks are about as happy as they make up their minds to be.

ABRAHAM LINCOLN

No matter where you are today, or what you have done or not done in the past, you need to accept seven essential truths about you as a person:

1. You are a thoroughly *good and excellent person*; valuable and worthwhile beyond measure. No one is better than you or more gifted than you.

   Only when you *doubt* your essential goodness and value do you begin to question yourself. The inability to accept that you are a good person lies at the root of much of your discontent.

2. *You are important*, in many, many ways. To start with, you are important to yourself. Your personal universe revolves around you as an individual. You give meaning to everything that you see or hear. Nothing in your world has any significance except for the significance that *you* attribute to it.

   You are also important to your parents. Your birth was a significant moment in their lives, and as you grew up, almost everything you did was meaningful to them.

   You are important to your own family, to your partner or spouse, your children, and the other members of your social circle. Some of the things you do or say have an enormous impact on them.

   You are important to your company, your customers, your coworkers, and your community. The things you do or don't do can have a tremendous effect on the lives and work of others.

   How important you feel largely determines the quality of your life. Happy, successful people feel important and valuable. Because they feel and act this way, it becomes true for them.

Unhappy, frustrated people feel unimportant and of little value. They feel frustrated and unworthy. They feel "I'm not good enough," and as a result they lash out at the world and engage in behaviors that hurt themselves and others.

They don't realize that they could be a prince or princess inside.

3. *You have unlimited potential* and the ability to create your life and your world as you desire. You could not use your entire potential if you lived one hundred lifetimes.

No matter what you have accomplished up to now, it is merely a hint of what is truly possible for you. And the more of your natural talents and abilities you develop in the present, the more of your potential you can develop in the future.

Your belief in your almost unlimited potential is the key to becoming everything you are truly capable of becoming.

4. *You create your world* in every respect by the way you think and the depth of your convictions. Your beliefs actually create your realities, and every belief you have about yourself you *learned*, starting in infancy. The amazing thing is that most of the negative or self-limiting beliefs and doubts that interfere with your happiness and success are not based on fact or reality at all.

When you begin to question your self-limiting beliefs and develop beliefs consistent with the incredible person you really are, your life will begin to change almost immediately.

5. *You are always free to choose* the content of your thoughts and the direction of your life. The one thing over which you have complete control is your inner life and your thinking. You can decide to think happy, fulfilling, uplifting thoughts that lead to positive actions and results. Or you can, by default, end up choosing negative, self-limiting thoughts that trip you up and hold you back.

   Your mind is like a garden: if you do not deliberately cultivate flowers, weeds will grow automatically without any effort on your part. If you do not deliberately plant and cultivate positive thoughts, negative thoughts will grow in their place.

   This simple metaphor about the garden explains why so many people are unhappy and don't know why.

6. You are put on this earth with a *great destiny*: you are meant to do something wonderful with your life. You have a unique combination of talents, abilities, ideas, insights, and experiences that make you different from anyone who has ever lived. You are designed for success and engineered for greatness.

   Your acceptance or nonacceptance of this point largely determines the size of the goals you set, your power of persistence in the face of adversity, the height of your achievements, and the whole direction of your life.

7. *There are no limits* to what you can do, be, or have except the limits you place on your own thinking and your own

imagination. The biggest enemies you will ever face are your own doubts and fears. These are usually negative beliefs, not necessarily based on fact, that you have accepted over the years until you no longer question them.

As Shakespeare wrote in *The Tempest*, "What's past is prologue." Everything that has happened to you in the past has been a preparation for the wonderful life that lies ahead of you in the future.

Remember the rule: *It doesn't matter where you're coming from; all that really matters is where you're going.*

Michelangelo's *David*

In the Gallery of the Academy in Florence, Italy, stands the *David*, by Michelangelo, considered by many to be the most beautiful piece of sculpture in the world.

It is said that later in his life, Michelangelo was once asked how he was able to sculpt something so beautiful. He explained that he was walking to his studio one morning and he happened to glance down a side street to where a huge block of marble, brought down from the mountains some years ago, was lying, overgrown with grass and bushes.

He had walked this way many times, but this time, he stopped and examined the huge block of marble, walking around it several times. Suddenly, he realized that this was exactly what he had been seeking to create the statue that had been commissioned. He had the block brought to his studio, where he worked on it for almost four years to create the *David*.

As legend has it, he said later, "I saw the *David* in the block of marble at the very beginning. My sole job from then on was to remove everything that was *not* the *David*, until only perfection was left."

This Is Your Story

In the same sense, you may be like the *David* imprisoned in the marble. The great goal of your life is to remove all those fears, doubts, insecurities, negative emotions, and false beliefs that hold you back until what remains is only the very best person you could possibly be.

Your job is to "kiss that frog" and find the positive elements that exist within every situation, to deliberately turn every negative into a positive, and to unleash the "handsome prince" in your own life.

Make a decision, right now, that you are going to unlock your full potential for success and happiness and become the extraordinary person that lies deep within you. You are going to accomplish all the wonderful things that you were put in this world to achieve. In the pages ahead, you will learn how.

NOW DO THIS

Identify the negative or self-limiting beliefs about your personal abilities or your situation that might be holding you back. Then ask yourself, "What if they weren't true?"

What if you had all the talent and ability that you could ever need to achieve almost anything in life? What if you had no limitations? What goals would you set for yourself if you were guaranteed of success, and what would you do differently starting today?

2

Imagine Your Handsome Prince

The princess did not start off dreaming about marrying whoever came along. She began with a clear idea of meeting a handsome prince who would be ideal for her in every respect. What is your handsome prince or princess in your work or your personal life?

To become a truly happy and fulfilled person, you must start with a clear definition of the ideal person you would like to be and the perfect life you would like to live. What qualities and characteristics would you have if you were the very best person you could possibly be?

Psychologists have described fully functioning, self-actualizing people as *genuinely happy, at peace with the world and themselves, self-confident, positive, personable, relaxed, feeling that they are fulfilling their full potential, grateful, energized, and generally feeling terrific about life.* If this description is a good goal for you in the months ahead, this book will show you how to become that kind of person.

Dream no small dreams for they have no power to move the hearts of men.

WOLFGANG VON GOETHE

The Magic Wand Exercise

Practice the "magic wand" exercise. As you think into the future, imagine that you could wave a magic wand and make your life ideal in the four critical areas that determine much of your happiness or unhappiness: (1) income and career, (2) family and relationships, (3) health and fitness, and (4) financial independence.

One of the most important behaviors of successful people is called "idealization." In idealizing, you create a vision of a perfect future for yourself in every area of your life. You practice "no limit" thinking.

Imagine that you have all the time and money, all the friends and contacts, all the education and experience, and all the talents and abilities that you could possibly need to *be, have, or do* anything. If this were your situation, what would you really want to do with your life?

When you combine idealization with the magic wand exercise, you liberate your mind from the constraints of day-to-day work and bill paying. You practice what is called "blue sky" thinking, a hallmark of top people and peak performers in every area.

Design Your Perfect Future

Practice "back-from-the-future" thinking. Project forward five years, and look back to where you are today. Write down your answers to the following questions:

1. If your job, career, or business were perfect in five years, how would it look? How much would you be earning?

How would your situation be different from what it is today?

Why aren't you already living this life and enjoying your ideal career and income?

2. If your family and relationships, your home and lifestyle, were perfect in five years, how would they look? And how would they be different from what they are today?

What is the first step that you could take to begin creating this ideal home life?

3. If your levels of health and fitness were perfect in five years, how would you look and feel? How much would you weigh? How much would you exercise each day or week? What foods would you eat? And especially, how would you be different physically from the person you are today?

What is the first thing you could start doing, or stop doing, to enjoy perfect health and fitness?

4. Finally, if your financial situation were perfect in five years, how much would you be worth? How much would you have in the bank, and how much would you be earning from your investments each month and each year?

What is the first step you could take?

Plan Your Perfect Day

Often when Christina spends the day with her husband she asks him, "If this were your perfect day, what would you do with it?" She asks the same question of herself. Then they find a way to combine their two perfect days.

If at the start they gave in to the fact that they would have to compromise, they would be restricted in how they defined their perfect days. But when each defines what would be perfection, their pictures are completely different.

In life, we often start off by thinking about all the restrictions and limitations that must be taken into account. However, if you start off by imagining that you have no limitations, you will be amazed at what you come up with. The rule is this: Decide what's ideal before you decide what's possible.

Most of all, what do you have to do, starting today, to prepare for the ideal future that you desire?

 ## NOW DO THIS

Dream big. Start with a clear definition of the ideal person you would like to be and the perfect life you would like to live.

Imagine that you have a magic wand to wave over your career, family and relationships, health and fitness, and financial situation. How would you make each of these perfect?

Practice "no limit" thinking. Liberate your mind from day-to-day challenges by practicing "blue sky" thinking.

Decide what's ideal before you decide what's possible.

Design your ideal future so that you can begin to take complete control of your life.

Decide upon the one goal, that if you could achieve it within twenty-four hours, would have the greatest positive impact on your life.

Resolve to take one action immediately to begin creating your ideal life.

3

Look Your Frog in the Face

When the beautiful princess was asked to kiss that wet, slimy, cold, ugly frog, she had a choice to make. She could continue in her current situation, alone and unhappy, or she could summon up her courage and take a chance with the frog, even though there were no guarantees.

All of us have a frog that we need to kiss, sometimes several frogs. The frogs in your life are negative people, situations, and past experiences; current problems; and your doubts and self-limiting beliefs. Some frogs are risks and commitments you have to make if you want to get unstuck and move ahead.

Face the Facts

Sometimes, to kiss your frog, you are really deciding to *embrace* the frog and accept that frogs can be slimy, cold, and ugly. Sometimes you are kissing the frog good-bye and letting go of a judgmental or guilt-provoking frog. Sometimes you are choosing to change your

Denial ain't just a river in Egypt.

MARK TWAIN

17

expectations and see the frog in a new way. Other times you may need to kiss the frog on the forehead and forgive it. There are many ways to eliminate frogs from your life.

The world of psychology has identified two types of personalities: the "confronter" and the "evader." Not surprisingly, *confronters*, people who face their fears, confront their reality, and deal honestly and straightforwardly with the people and problems in their lives, are much happier, more effective, and more self-confident than *evaders*.

Confronters acknowledge and face the fear involved in confronting. They take charge of their emotions. Evaders fear the unknown and lack the trust in themselves that is necessary to move ahead.

Fortunately, you can become a more powerful and positive person by resolving to "look your frog in the face before you kiss it"—by making it a habit to confront your situation honestly rather than to evade it or deny that you have a problem in the first place.

Be Realistic

In her counseling practice, Christina often deals with clients who are constantly disappointed by frustrated expectations. One young woman in her thirties would have her sessions after visiting her parents and talk about how upset she was that they would put out only limited effort to spend time with her when she made the effort to visit.

She discussed with Christina what she expected her parents to do when she went for a visit and worked to change her expectations. Once she decided that she would *lower* her expectations, she stopped being disappointed and her feelings toward her parents improved. She experienced her frog differently. By deliberately changing her expectations, she changed how she felt and took control of her emotions.

One of the truisms that everyone eventually learns is "People don't change." Their basic personalities and attitudes solidify around the age of seventeen or eighteen and remain much the same for the rest of their lives. For this reason, it is always an exercise in frustration to try to get others to change.

This does not mean that people cannot develop new skills and abilities and become more of what they are truly capable of becoming, but in the absence of a real desire to change accompanied by hard work, very little change ever takes place.

The main point is that you must never sacrifice your own happiness or peace of mind by wishing and hoping that someone will change from what he or she has always been into someone else, someone who is more suitable to you. It is probably never going to happen.

Deal with Reality

Denial, or the refusal to face the truth or reality of your situation or of another person, is a major source of stress, anxiety, negative emotions, and even physical and mental illness. The opposite of denial is *acceptance*. When you accept that a person or situation, at home or at work, is the way it is and is not going to change and act accordingly, most of the stress generated by the situation fades away.

Separate Facts from Problems

Many negative emotions are triggered by an inappropriate *overreaction* to an unexpected setback or difficulty. It is vital that you carefully analyze a problem when it occurs to ensure that you thoroughly understand it and what you can do to deal with it or resolve it. Here's how to begin.

First, make the distinction between a fact and a problem. The difference is simple. A fact is something that is *unchangeable*. Your age is a fact. The weather is a fact. Certain things just *are*. They cannot be altered. They are facts.

One of the keys to happiness is to resolve to never become upset or angry about a fact. Just as you do not become angry at physical things, like a piece of furniture because you bumped into it, you do not become angry or upset about facts. You simply accept them and adjust your life and activities around them.

What, then, is a problem? A problem is something you can do something about. A goal unachieved is a problem unsolved. An obstacle in your path is a problem unsolved. You can focus your intelligence and ability on solving problems and achieving goals. Problems are simply challenges that you deal with as you go through life.

The Past and the Future

There are two time periods in your life: the past and the future. The present is a single moment passing between the two. Into what category of time do we put facts, and into what category do we put problems?

The truth is that most facts that make you unhappy exist in the *past*. Something that happened in the past is a fact. It is unchangeable. This is important to understand because many people are miserable and unhappy in the present because of something that did not work out the way they expected it to sometime in the past. But because it happened, or didn't happen, in the past, it is now an unchangeable fact. It does no good to be upset about a fact.

A problem exists in the future. A problem is an issue that you can do something about. This is an area where you can focus your intelligence and ability into achieving a different result. A problem, the future, is under your control, and its outcome is determined by what you do in the present.

A Rained-Out Picnic

Imagine that you run into a man at a social function and ask him, "How are you doing?" He replies with a sour look and says, "I am doing fine, but I am still really angry about what happened."

A bit surprised, you ask, "What happened?"

He says, "Well, about five years ago, my family and I packed a picnic basket on Saturday night so that we could go out and have a nice picnic on Sunday. But on Sunday morning, it was overcast and it rained for the whole day, so we had to cancel the picnic. And I'm still mad."

At about this time, you would probably be thinking, "This person needs a *checkup* from the *neck up*. He is not thinking rationally. How could he still be angry about the fact that it rained five years ago?"

The Gunnysacker

This may sound ridiculous, but many people today are still angry, upset, and even dysfunctional in their relationships and work because of a past event that cannot be changed. They are still mad or sad today because of a relationship that went sour years ago, an investment that lost money, or a job that didn't work out for whatever reason.

Instead of accepting the situation, they practice what is called "gunnysacking," carrying it around with them, ready to pull it out and show to anyone who expresses interest. (You often meet them at social gatherings or sit next to them on airplanes.)

When Christina is working with clients who are struggling to let go of a past experience or setback, rather than pushing them to let go and move past whatever pet frog they've become attached to, she asks "How does it serve you to hold on to this issue/excuse/feeling?" This is a powerful question. We often hold on to a negative because it protects us from taking a chance on something new, such as taking a risk in a relationship or new business activity.

One of the hallmarks of happy, well-balanced people is that they look past their problems, their ugly frogs, straight in the eye, accept them as past events that cannot be changed, learn what they can from them, and then get so busy working on their lives and work that they don't have any time to think about them.

Analyze the Situation

One way that you can take control of a negative situation is by analyzing it carefully. You do this by *asking questions*. It is not possible for you to become or remain upset, angry, and out of control when you are asking questions and seeking to understand the situation or the change that has taken place. Here are four questions you can ask to take control of any situation:

1. *"What exactly happened?"* At this stage, be patient. Strive for accuracy. Refuse to attack or blame someone or something for what has occurred. Instead, focus on clarity and understanding. Resolve to remain calm and unemotional.

2. *"How did it happen?"* Imagine that you are gathering evidence for a third party; you are more concerned with accuracy than with recrimination. Ask follow-up questions so that you thoroughly understand the details.

3. *"What can be done?"* Take control of your thinking by focusing on the future, on what can be done, rather than what has happened, which cannot be changed. This makes you more positive and puts you in control of your emotions and of the situation.

4. *"What actions will we take now?"* Instead of worrying or wallowing in pity or remorse, get busy taking whatever actions you can to resolve the situation and move forward.

Seek to Understand

Stephen Covey, in his book *The 7 Habits of Highly Effective People*, said, "Seek first to understand, then to be understood." Focus on understanding the situation clearly before you make any judgment or come to any conclusions.

Avoid the tendency to "catastrophize," to think or assume the very worst in a difficult situation. Very few things are ever as bad as they first appear.

Avoid the common mistake of confusing *correlation* with *causation*, of assuming that if two events occur at the same time, one of the events caused the other. This thinking error can lead to your jumping to conclusions—and to *false* conclusions at that. In many cases, two events happening together are merely coincidence. Neither of the events has anything to do with the other.

The key to analyzing a situation is to continue to ask questions and gather information. Sometimes, what appears to be a major setback or problem turns out not to be as serious as you thought. Often, what initially seems to be a problem is an opportunity to make a change, which is often a blessing in disguise.

The practice of acceptance rather than denial, of confronting rather than evading, of looking a frog in the face rather than pretending that it is not as unpleasant as it may be, are the hallmarks of the effective person. People who respond positively and constructively to the inevitable ups and downs of their work and personal lives are the most respected in every organization.

The Worry Buster

One of the best ways to eliminate worry is to use the "Worry Buster" on any situation that causes you stress or anxiety. There are four steps to using the Worry Buster method:

Step one: Define the worry situation *clearly*. What exactly are you worrying about?

Many people are worrying about something vague. Their thinking is confused. Like children in the night, they experience feelings of anxiety for reasons about which they are unclear. Or they do not have sufficient information, which can cause them to overreact.

In medicine, it is said, "Accurate diagnosis is half the cure." The very act of defining your worry situation clearly, in writing if possible, will often suggest an immediate solution that eliminates the worry situation completely.

Step two: Determine the *worst possible outcome* of this worry situation. What is the worst thing that could possibly happen?

Most negative emotions and worry situations are caused by *denial*. People feel an enormous amount of stress because they deny the reality of a situation. They do not want it to be true. They hope that by ignoring it, it will go away or it will not be as serious. But this approach seldom works.

When you identify the worst thing that could possibly happen as a result of this problem situation, you often find that the potential outcome is not as bad as you thought. It may be the end of a relationship, but it won't kill you. It may be the loss of a certain amount of money, but it won't bankrupt you. Even if it does bankrupt you, the worry situation is a fact, not a problem, and has to be faced. You'll earn the money back at a later time, doing something different, in a different way and a different place. Think positively.

If the situation involves a health problem, resolve to confront it squarely. Refuse to play games with yourself. Do whatever you can to resolve the problem, and then trust your health to the experts and to a higher power.

Step three: Resolve to *accept* the worst, should it occur. Since most stress is caused by a refusal to identify and accept the worst possible outcome, once you resolve to accept the worst, should it occur, your stress disappears. You suddenly feel calm and at peace. When you replace denial with acceptance, you take full mental and emotional control of the situation.

Step four: Begin immediately to *improve* upon the worst. Do everything that you possibly can to minimize the damage, control the costs, and cut your losses. Become so busy taking action to resolve your difficulties that you don't have any time left to worry.

 NOW DO THIS

Think of a recent setback that you experienced and ask yourself the following four questions. Observe yourself as you answer these questions and see if the process changes your experience of the situation.

What exactly happened?

How did it happen?

What can be done?

What actions will we take now?

4

Clear the Pond of Ugly Frogs

Your goal in life is to be happy. Happiness and peace of mind are the ultimate aim of almost all individuals. Your ability to achieve your own happiness is the real measure of how successful you are as a human being.

The good news is that it has never been more possible for you to achieve happiness and fulfillment in every part of your life than it is today. We know more today about the reasons for happiness and unhappiness than we have ever known before. We have learned more about the functioning of the human brain relative to happiness, and to all other functions, in the last few years than we ever knew before.

When Brian was in his twenties, ambitious and eager to live a happy, fulfilling life, he began to study the subject of happiness. After thousands of hours of reading and research in the areas of psychology, philosophy,

The truth is that all of us attain the greatest success and happiness possible in this life whenever we use our native capacities to their greatest extent.

SMILEY BLANTON

religion, and success, he got an extraordinary insight into
the entire subject.

The Main Obstacle

He discovered that *negative emotions*, ugly frogs that squat
in the back of your mental pond, are the primary obstacles
to enjoying the happiness you truly desire. Negative emotions, from whatever source, are the root causes of almost all
the unhappiness, misery, and frustration in life and work.
If you can eliminate negative emotions, you can transform
your whole life!

He also learned that the mind is like a *vacuum*. It will not
remain empty for very long. When you eliminate negative
emotions, your mind will refill naturally with positive emotions of happiness, joy, excitement, love, and peace. When
you get rid of the weeds, flowers will grow.

Sometimes, a single new idea or insight that leads to your
interpreting a past event differently can liberate you so completely that you will never be the same in that area. Forever
after, you will be a different person.

Negatives Sometimes Turn into Positives

For example, you could get fired from a job and be angry
at your employer for the injustice of it all. Then you find a
new and better job that is much more suited to your special talents and abilities, you work with people you really
enjoy, and the job pays far more than you could have ever
earned at the previous job. In retrospect, you realize that

your previous employer did you a huge favor by firing you, and instead of being angry, you think back with gratitude.

One of the most helpful habits you can develop is choosing to *seek the valuable lesson* in everything that happens to you, especially negative experiences. When you have an unexpected setback or temporary failure (a cold, slimy frog), decide that, since you have complete control of your thoughts, you will seek the lesson or benefit that you can gain from the situation. Very often, you can gain insights, ideas, confidence, and new opportunities. What is the most valuable lesson contained in your biggest difficulty or problem right now?

Take Control of Your Mind

To become the best person you can possibly be, you need to start at the beginning. The Law of Control says that you feel happy about yourself to the degree to which you feel you are *in control* of your own life, and you feel unhappy to the degree to which you feel you are *not in control* or are controlled by external circumstances or people.

You have either an internal locus of control, where you feel in charge of your own life, or you have an external locus of control, where you feel that you are controlled by circumstances and people—your boss, your bills, your health—that you can do nothing about. Psychologists today agree that the presence or absence of a sense of control is the critical factor in stress or lack of stress, happiness or unhappiness, and almost every human malady, mental and emotional.

The fact is that you have complete control over only one thing—your mind. You can control the thoughts you think. As Victor Frankl, survivor of the Auschwitz concentration camp, said, "The last of the human freedoms—to choose one's attitude in any given set of circumstances, to choose one's own way."

Your single focus must then be the *elimination* of negative emotions of all kinds. Fortunately, negative emotions can be eliminated and removed by using a series of proven methods and techniques, many of which can act in seconds, which you will learn in the pages ahead.

 NOW DO THIS

Starting today, begin paying attention to your thoughts when situations upset you, frustrate you, or invoke negative feelings. Take a deep breath and make the decision not to *feed* them. In *Emotional Intelligence,* Daniel Goleman talks about a process that some people refer to as "emotional snowballing." The negative emotion starts off small, but the more energy and attention you give it, the greater it becomes. Choose to dwell on positive thoughts and feelings and starve the negative ones. Remember, you are in control of your thoughts!

Program Yourself to Be Optimistic

Where do your emotions come from? Which comes first, the thought or the feeling? The fact is that *thought precedes feeling,* and feeling precedes decision and action. First you think a thought or take in new information. You then interpret that thought as being either positive or negative. Your interpretation then generates the appropriate emotion. The emotion then triggers an action or a reaction on your part.

Put another way, you determine your emotional life and much of what happens to you by the way you *choose* to think about an event or experience. You are the one who gives *meaning* to each part of your life—no one else.

The way that most people think is based on the stimulus-response model of behavioral psychology. A particular stimulus or event can trigger a particular response or reaction almost instantly. Much of your thinking and feeling is automatic and instinctive, where you simply react as you have done over and over in the past.

However, the best thinkers, the happiest and most successful people, think and respond *differently* from average people. Instead of immediately responding to a stimulus, the most effective people take the time to think about what is happening and the best way to respond. In those moments of thought between the stimulus and the response, the quality of individual life is determined.

The Power of Thoughtfulness

When you develop the habit of thinking in a positive and constructive way about the events in your life *before* you respond, you will make better choices and decisions and take more constructive actions than those who simply react with little thought about the consequences.

When you look back over your life, you will see that many of your mistakes that caused unhappiness and grief were the result of not having given the subject enough thought before you acted.

The Law of Substitution

The Law of Substitution says that you can hold only *one thought* in your mind at a time, positive or negative. It also says that you can deliberately *substitute* a positive thought for a negative thought. You can choose to think a thought that makes you positive or happy in place of any thought that makes you unhappy.

Dr. Martin Seligman of the University of Pennsylvania conducted twenty-two years of research into the subject of optimism. One of his most important conclusions was that people are optimistic or pessimistic depending upon their "explanatory style."

Your explanatory style is how you *interpret* events to yourself. Each person can have her own perception or interpretation of an event or situation, and whatever her perception, her feelings happen automatically as a result of her interpretation. Perception is *reality*. That's why it is said that there are always three sides to a story, the first person's version, the second person's, and what actually occurred.

You Can Reinterpret a Situation

In a similar vein, the field of neurolinguistic programming refers to "framing" and "reframing." The situation itself is not what causes you to feel happy or unhappy. It is your interpretation of the situation as being either positive or negative that triggers the corresponding emotion. By re-framing a past experience, you will find that your emotional response will totally shift and relieve you of old negative feelings.

For example, when you first look at a cold, slimy frog (or any difficult person or situation) and imagine touching it or being near it, you may feel repulsed. However, if you rein-terpret it and think about the fact that frogs eat mosquitoes and mosquito bites are awfully uncomfortable, you may see the frog with new appreciation.

Reframing is a major tool in psychotherapy. Often if peo-ple can develop another perspective on their situation, their feelings toward it change completely. If you are unhappy because you had a difficult childhood and you begin to think how your childhood experiences combined to make you a better person as an adult, you can change your per-spective. You can actually be grateful for the difficulties you had growing up because they made you the excellent per-son you are today.

Language is very important in this area. The words that you choose to use to interpret an event can trigger thoughts, feelings, emotions, and reactions, positive or negative. Choose your words with care.

Brian's Story

Brian came from a poor home with no money and few opportunities. He didn't graduate from high school. He worked at laboring jobs for several years, washing dishes, and digging ditches and wells. In his midtwenties, he got into sales, where he eventually succeeded, and then into sales management, where he succeeded even more. By the time he reached the age of thirty, his life was turning around and he was on the way up in his career.

As his fortunes improved, he one day took a deep breath and bought his dream car, a two-year-old Mercedes-Benz 450 SEL, silver-gray with blue leather upholstery. He was able to trade in his older car as the down payment and had to stretch the monthly payments over five years, but at last he had the car he had always wanted.

When he took it out on the highway, he would step on the accelerator, and it would start moving like a big boat, faster and faster until he had to slow down to avoid getting speeding tickets. After he had driven this big, powerful car for a year, he took it in for servicing by a mechanic who specialized in Mercedes-Benz repairs.

One Small Part

When he picked up the car, the mechanic, Mario, said that he had found a problem in the carburetor. A previous mechanic had inserted a key part backward, thereby cutting down the amount of fuel going into the engine. Mario had replaced this part with a new part and installed it properly. He said, "Step on the gas carefully; you will notice the difference."

Brian was already quite content with his car. It seemed to drive fine and went as fast as he dared on the open highway. But this time, when he barely touched the gas pedal, the car exploded forward as though propelled by a rocket. He had to slam on the brakes to keep from crashing into the traffic on the street.

From then on, whenever he drove his Mercedes, Brian had to step on the accelerator very gently. A slight touch would cause that car to blast forward at such a speed, zero to 60 miles per hour in five seconds, that he would have to brake quickly to hold it back. And all because of changing one small part deep in the carburetor.

You Have Extraordinary Abilities

Your mind and potential are like a beautifully engineered Mercedes. Even if your life is moving along in a satisfactory or even fairly successful way, you may have, deep within your mind, a negative memory or block, an ugly frog, holding you back from accomplishing extraordinary things with your life. When you identify this block and remove it, you will suddenly begin to make more progress in a few weeks or months than you might have made in several years.

In the next chapter, you will learn how to identify those hidden blocks that hold you back. You will learn how to release vast reserves of energy, enthusiasm, and desire in a direction of your own choosing. You will learn proven ideas and insights that can change your life.

NOW DO THIS

Identify one area where you might still be harboring anger at a person from your past or still be thinking about a negative experience that could be holding you back from putting your whole heart into your work or personal life.

Resolve today that you are going to reinterpret the negative experience in a positive way, learn from it, let it go, and then focus your entire attention on your goals and the future rather than continuing to think about the past.

5

Drain the Swamp

Everyone wants to be happy and self-fulfilled. Everyone wants to experience joy, satisfaction, happy relationships, and peace of mind. Why, then, are so many people, by their own admission, leading "lives of quiet desperation"?

In almost every case, as we have discussed, the lack of happiness and personal fulfillment can be traced back to negative emotions and the blocks they throw in the paths of our lives. Those ugly frogs deep in the mental swamp trip us up and hold us back.

Because of destructive criticism and a lack of sufficient love in childhood, children can begin to develop negative emotions at an early age. As they become adults, these emotions

People are always blaming circumstances for what they are. I don't believe in circumstances. The people who get on in this world are the people who get up and look for the circumstances they want, and if they can't find them, make them.

VIVIE WARREN, *MRS. WARREN'S PROFESSION*, GEORGE BERNARD SHAW can become more and more intense and generate additional negative emotions of various kinds.

The main negative emotions that people experience are fear, doubt, worry, envy, jealousy, hate, resentment, undeservingness, and feelings of inadequacy, especially in comparison to others.

Fear, doubt, and worry arise when a child is continually criticized. Even if he accomplishes something worthwhile, it is never enough to satisfy his parents. In many homes, the parents seldom express love or approval, or they immediately withdraw their love and approval if they feel that the child is failing to please them in some way.

Emotions Distort Evaluations

All emotions, especially negative emotions, distort evaluations. A person in the grip of a negative emotion is incapable of thinking clearly or rationally. The more intense the negative emotion, the more the sufferer becomes detached from reality and is incapable of reasoning clearly. The person then talks and acts in a way that is often unexplainable and destructive.

Some years ago, Abigail Trafford, a New York writer who had been through a particularly bitter divorce, wrote *Crazy Time*. In the book, she explained how the emotionally chaotic two years of her divorce caused her to behave in ways that she could barely recognize when the divorce was over and she returned to normal. She felt that she had been "insane" for the entire time because of the intensity of the negativity she was feeling. Many people have similar experiences when going through an emotionally stressful situation. Emotions distort evaluations.

The Roots of Negative Emotions

Five major factors cause people to create negative emotions and hold on to them. These are some of the worst frogs of all, swimming deep in the darkest waters of the emotional swamp. They are *justification, identification, hypersensitivity, judgmentalism,* and *rationalization.* To free yourself from negative emotions, you must recognize where they come from so that you can get rid of them or even stop them from developing in the first place.

Justification

With *justification,* you defend your negativity and your *right* to be angry. Negative emotions cannot exist unless you can justify your right to experience them to yourself and others.

When you are discussing a particular negative situation, you become preoccupied with justifying your negativity on a variety of grounds. Often you talk to yourself as you drive, making your case and arguing vehemently with people who are not there. Justification often keeps you awake at night.

The more you justify yourself and convince yourself that the other person involved is *bad* in some way, that you are pure and innocent and are therefore entitled to feel the way you do, the angrier and more upset you become.

Although a situation may have occurred that hurt you, angered you, or was unjust, the only person who can attach an emotion to that experience is you. You can choose to hold on or let go.

Identification

The second key requirement for negative emotions is *identification*. This means that you take things *personally*. You interpret what has happened as a personal attack on you.

If you cannot personally identify with a negative situation, you will have difficulty generating any emotion, positive or negative, about it. If you read in the paper that a thousand people—men, women, and children—had been washed away and drowned by a flood in northern China, you would feel some remorse and then probably flip the page to the next subject with little or no emotion. Because you do not know any of the people affected or even know much about that part of the world, you do not *identify* with the tragedy. As a result, you experience no negative emotions about it.

This does not mean you can't feel compassion for someone else's experience or hurt, but you do not become emotionally involved. For example, if a coworker is not keeping up on her tasks due to some personal problems, you may feel bad for her, but that does not make it your job to take on her responsibilities at a cost to yourself. Having healthy emotional boundaries is essential, especially in a work environment. You can be compassionate without identifying with someone else's emotions.

Hypersensitivity

The third cause of negative emotions is *hypersensitivity* to the thoughts, opinions, or attitudes of others toward you.

As we mentioned earlier, people who have been raised with destructive criticism and insufficient love can develop deep feelings of inferiority and inadequacy. These feelings will manifest in a concern about the actions, reactions, and treatment that they experience from other people.

Peter Ouspensky, in his book *In Search of the Miraculous*, referred to this process as "inward considering," or feeling extremely sensitive to the way you are treated by other people or even feeling upset and depressed because you *think* that someone else is thinking negatively about you.

One positive word or comment of approval from another person can cause you to be elated. One negative glance can crush you. Truly hypersensitive people often see slight and disapproval where none exist. In extreme cases, hypersensitive people become paralyzed in that they cannot make a decision without getting the approval of other people.

Judgmentalism

The fourth reason for negative emotions is *judgmentalism*, the tendency of people to make negative assessments about others. When you judge others unfavorably, you invariably find them *guilty* of something. This guilt becomes the justification for your anger and resentment and negative feelings toward them.

The Bible (Matt. 7:1) says, "Judge not, that ye be not judged." When you judge others, you actually bring negativity and unhappiness upon yourself. Whatever measure you use to judge others will be the measure they use to judge you. When you judge others, you are setting yourself up as someone who is superior to them, making them inferior to you and often triggering a negative reaction from them.

If you do not pass judgment on another, for any reason, you cannot become angry at that person. You can be angry only when you can make a good case to yourself that the other person has done or said something, or failed to do something, that has hurt you.

To start eliminating judgmentalism from your life, resolve, from now on, not to judge anyone else for anything. This is very hard to do, especially at the beginning, but you will get better at it with practice. Just keep reminding yourself that all people are entitled to their own way of thinking and living.

NOW DO THIS

Very often we judge others because we see something in them that we don't like in ourselves or we are jealous of them and want to be able to achieve the same results or enjoy the same rewards as they do. The next time you find yourself passing judgment on someone, explore your motivation. Do you dislike or suspect a similar trait in yourself? Or do you long to have the qualities and lifestyle that the other person has?

Judging and Condemning   The opposite of judging and condemning is neutrality, remaining unemotional and unattached to the person or situation. You achieve this state with the Buddhist practice of *detachment*. Remain calm and unemotional. Stand back from the person, and allow him to be who he is and do what he does without measuring him by your own personal values and standards. In most cases, his actions don't concern you at all.

When you judge another, you become emotional. And emotions distort evaluations. The more you judge and condemn, the angrier and more negative you become. People often judge others because they want to control their behavior. The reality is that again, all people are entitled to live their own lives in their own way, as long as it does not negatively affect the lives of others. Live and let live.

If you were brought up in a family where someone was continually complaining about or criticizing others, you may have the false idea that judging and condemning others is a normal and natural behavior. The very idea of remaining neutral and detached when someone does or says something that you don't agree with may sound strange to you.

You have a wonderful mind. But it is a two-edged sword. You can use it to make yourself happy, or you can use it to make yourself angry. Your goal should be to use your intelligence to keep yourself calm, in control, and at peace, no matter what is happening around you or to you.

When people behave poorly, refrain from judging them. When people do or say things that seem to be negative and unnecessary, stand back and observe them impartially, without becoming upset or involved.

NOW DO THIS

For twenty-four hours, resolve to refrain from judging anyone for anything. Remain neutral. See how hard it is to practice detachment after it has become a habit to judge others continually!

Feel Sorry for Others The best way to stop yourself from judging is to *pity* or *empathize* with the other person. It is almost impossible to pity another person and judge that person negatively at the same time. Even better, you can *bless, forgive, and let go.* Rise above the situation. Refuse to allow the behavior of the other person to affect you in any way. Use the Law of Substitution to start thinking about something that makes you happy, thereby neutralizing the negative thought and any tendency to judge the other person.

When you deal with a difficult person, treat that person exactly as if he or she was a tired, hungry, irritable child who is becoming angry or even throwing a tantrum. You don't get angry with a child. You just accept that this is the way that children behave at certain times under certain circumstances. You may also pause and reflect on the times you felt tired, stressed, and difficult to be around. We all have our moments.

Another way to refrain from judging is to remind yourself that in a similar situation, you might act the same. You can say, "There, but for the grace of God, go I." You allow others to live their own lives in the same way you want to be allowed to live your own life.

The Sedona Method The Sedona Method, developed by Hale Dwoskin, is a way of regaining emotional control in your life. In this method, you identify the people in your past with whom you are still angry. In addition, you identify the situations from your past that you are still upset about.

You then answer two questions. The first question is, "Do you want to be free of the negativity associated with this situation?" If your answer is yes, the second question is, "Are you willing to let it go completely?"

It is surprising how many people are *not* willing to let go of a negative experience that happened to them in the past. They feel that they have earned it and paid for it with time, money, and personal suffering. They feel entitled to their pain. In their heart of hearts, they are not willing to let it go.

Let It Go   Here is the example given by the instructors of the Sedona Method. Put a pencil in your hand. Squeeze the pencil tightly. Squeeze it as hard as you can.

Then turn your hand over with the palm facing toward the floor while you are squeezing this pencil. Here's the question: "What is holding this pencil in your hand?"

The answer is obvious. *You* are holding the pencil by squeezing it so hard.

The next question is "How do you get rid of this pencil?" And the answer is simple: you simply open your hand and let it fall.

This is a wonderful illustration of the simplicity of dropping a negative event out of your life permanently. With the pencil, you open your hand and let it go. With a negative experience that still makes you unhappy, you open your heart and let it go.

Remember, *no one makes you feel anything.* No one makes you mad. Nothing that has happened to you has any control over you. No event, circumstance, or person from your past can affect your emotions without your permission. The only one who makes you feel anything is you—by the way that you interpret a past event to yourself. The dead frogs in your slimy pond are just that: dead. You keep the negative emotions alive by feeding them with thought and energy. Decide today to let go of those frogs and get on with your life.

Practice Compassion with Others   One of the most beautiful emotions is that of *compassion*. Compassion means feeling the same emotions that another person is feeling and therefore understanding those emotions. It means feeling empathy for the other person and for the situation. You cannot experience a negative emotion of any kind toward another person when your heart goes out to that person in his or her difficult situation.

When you use your wonderful mind to *find reasons for not judging,* for letting the other person off the hook, and for letting go of any past hurt, you take complete control of your thinking. Instead of finding reasons why another person is guilty and should be condemned and punished, you instead seek reasons to find the other person "not guilty" and let him or her go free.

🐸 NOW DO THIS

Write down the names of all the people whom you are still angry with. Next to their names, write down what they did that causes you to feel justified in your anger and negative emotions. Now write down a list of reasons that they are not to blame, and decide to let them leave the swamp.

Now light this piece of paper on fire. Burn it ceremoniously in an ashtray, or throw it in a fire or barbeque. But let the flames destroy it completely.

In the same way, you can use your power of choice to let go of the hurt and pain of the past so that you can enjoy the freedom and happiness of the future.

Rationalization

Rationalization is what you do when you put a socially acceptable explanation on an otherwise socially unacceptable act. John Assaraf calls these "rational-lies."

Because of low self-esteem and weak egos, most people cannot admit that they have done or said anything that was not thoroughly reasonable and justified. Even the worst criminals feel that they are innocent and merely victims of someone, something, or society. They *rationalize* their behaviors.

Peter Ouspensky explained that almost all unhappiness comes from "the expression of negative emotions." The constant talking about and rehashing of a negative situation keeps the negative emotions alive and growing. In this sense, your negative emotions can be compared to a brush fire that begins with a small spark but quickly spreads out of control.

But if a spark lands on dry brush and you put it out immediately, no fire takes place or spreads. In the same way, if you stop the negative emotion the moment that it is triggered, it quickly goes out, like a small fire, and wreaks no damage.

Anger: The Core Negative Emotion

Sooner or later, all negative emotions come down to one: *anger*. Anger is the ultimate negative emotion. All fear, doubt, jealousy, envy, and resentment eventually turn into anger. This anger is then *inwardly* directed, making you sick physically and emotionally, or *outwardly* directed, undermining and destroying your relationships with other people.

All unhappy people are angry. *Depression* is inwardly directed anger, caused by the inability to express one's feelings about a situation openly and honestly. It is often triggered by feelings of low self-esteem and hopelessness.

Rage is outwardly directed anger, which takes the form of verbal or even physical attacks on other people for something they have done or not done.

The primary goal of psychological counseling is to help individuals process and understand their experiences, letting out the negative emotions that are holding them back. What many people discover in trying to understand their anger is that the anger is first sparked by hurt. When people can acknowledge that they feel hurt by something that someone did, didn't do, said, or didn't say, they find it much easier to release the emotional charge that keeps the anger alive.

The Roots of Anger

The primary reason for anger is feeling aggressed upon, attacked, hurt, or taken advantage of by another person. Anger is always rooted in defensiveness. Both anger and fear trigger the fight-or-flight response, causing the attacked person to withdraw for safety or to lash out at the attacker.

One of the worst aspects of anger is that the more someone expresses anger, the greater the anger grows, like a fire out of control. The reality is that the more someone feels angry, the greater the hurt becomes.

The expression of anger soon becomes a habit. The unhappy individual reaches the point where the smallest event triggers an explosion of anger. She goes through life angry most of the time. Soon, she comes to believe that her emotions and expressions of anger are a normal way to think and feel.

What compels people to persist in their anger is the need to have someone acknowledge the hurt and understand their pain. When listening to someone talk about something that makes that person mad or sad, perhaps the most helpful words you can say are "I understand exactly how you feel; if I was in your situation, I would feel the same way." Showing that you empathize is one of the fastest ways to calm an angry person. When people feel understood in their pain, they can start to heal.

The Centrality of Blame

The root cause of anger is *blame*. Blaming yourself or others for something that they have done or not done is the essential requirement for the feeling and expression of negative emotions of all kinds.

In fact, it is impossible to hold a negative emotion for any length of time unless you can blame someone or something for the situation that you are angry about. The moment that you stop blaming, the negative emotion stops simultaneously, like turning off a light switch.

The antidote to negative emotions is so simple and effective that it is almost overwhelming. People who have been negative, angry, and unhappy for years can short-circuit their negative emotions almost instantly with one simple but powerful decision: accept responsibility.

Three Magic Words

How do you accept responsibility? Simply say the words *"I am responsible!"*

Whenever you are angry or unhappy for any reason, you can immediately short-circuit the emotion by saying to yourself, over and over, "I am responsible! I am responsible! I am responsible!" until the negative feeling goes away. This is an astonishing discovery that totally transforms the life of every person who practices it.

Because of the Law of Substitution, your mind can hold only one thought at a time. It can hold the positive emotion of personal responsibility or it can hold the negative emotion of anger or blame. But it cannot hold both. And the choice is always up to you.

The only thing in the universe that you can control is the content of your conscious mind. If you choose to hold the positive thought "I am responsible" rather than the negative thought that makes you unhappy, you become positive, optimistic, and completely in control, sometimes in just a few moments.

You Are Responsible

Since all negative emotions are rooted in blame, the antidote is simple: instead of blaming, accept responsibility for the situation. When you *accept complete responsibility* for the situation, your negative emotions stop, like slamming on a brake. *It is impossible to accept responsibility for a situation and to simultaneously be angry or unhappy about that situation.* The acceptance of responsibility cancels out all the negativity associated with the situation (or person) and puts you back into emotional control.

For example, Christina had a client who had lost several jobs due to his explosive confrontations with coworkers and superiors. He was even-tempered most of the time, but because of his insecurities he would not speak up to gain clarification on projects. He allowed his frustration to boil to a point where he became explosive. In his work with Christina, he acknowledged and took responsibility for his role in losing his jobs. The two of them developed a plan for him to communicate his needs and concerns before he became overly frustrated, and as a result of his taking responsibility for his actions, he has remained at his current job for over two years.

Find Reasons Not to Express Negative Emotions

We said earlier that unhappiness comes from the expression of negative emotions—either to yourself or to others or both. If you do not express negative emotions, talk about them, or rehash them, you cannot feel negative.

From this moment onward, instead of using your incredible intelligence to think of reasons why you should be fearful, doubtful, envious, jealous, resentful, and angry because of things that have happened, use your creativity to *find reasons not to express* your negative feelings, justifications, and rationalizations.

The most powerful way to short-circuit the expression of negative emotions is to repeat "I am responsible!" every time an event occurs that would normally trigger a negative reaction from you.

At this point, many people say, "Wait a minute! There is no way that I can accept responsibility for the terrible thing that the other person did to hurt me. Accepting responsibility would not be honest because I am not responsible in any way."

You Can Control Your Responses

This may be true. You may have been robbed, cheated, lied to, swindled, betrayed, or hurt in countless ways by someone else. You may have gone to the parking lot and found that someone had banged into the side of your car and then driven away. In a case like this, you're not legally at fault and you are not to blame.

However, although you may not be responsible for what happened, you are responsible for the way that you behave *afterward*. Your response is completely under your control— totally a matter of personal choice. Nothing makes you angry or unhappy. You make *yourself* angry or unhappy by the way that you *choose* to react to the unhappy experience.

In the poem "If," Rudyard Kipling says, "If you can keep your head when all about you are losing theirs and blaming it on you; . . . you'll be a man, my son."

The mark of happy, effective people is that they exert their willpower and self-discipline to keep themselves calm and controlled no matter what is going on around them. Great men and women are those who have developed the ability to remain cool under fire.

Remember, *emotions distort evaluations*. The minute that you begin to blame someone else and become angry for what has occurred, you begin to lose your ability to think clearly and decide intelligently. You become a slave to your emotions. You can very quickly become swept away and find yourself doing and saying things that you later regret.

Get Over It

People who go though a bad relationship often remain furiously angry at the other person, sometimes for years, when the relationship breaks down. But when you say, "I am responsible!" and look for reasons why you were at least partially responsible, you will find that you made a lot of the decisions that got you into the bad relationship in the first place. You are not responsible for the actions of the other person, but you are fully responsible for everything that you did or said from the beginning of the relationship to the end and to the present day. You were not an innocent bystander.

You may become upset when a job doesn't work out or a business deal goes wrong. But you are responsible. No one forced you into the situation at gunpoint. Based on your knowledge and information, or lack of knowledge, you got yourself into the situation in the first place. Unfortunately, it did not work out as you expected. The next time you will be smarter and wiser. But for the moment, you are responsible.

Two Fires Burning

The Law of Emotion says that everything you do is determined by an emotion of some kind, either positive or negative. The emotions that you think about and talk about the most soon grow and consume your entire life and preoccupy your thinking, for better or worse.

Imagine that you have two fires burning. One is the *fire of desire* and the other is the *fire of negative emotions* based on your interpretation of past events.

You have a continuous flow of emotional energy, emotional *firewood*. You can put this wood on either fire. But if you put all the wood on one fire, what happens to the other fire?

The answer is simple. If you put all your emotions onto the fire of desire and spend all your time thinking and talking about what you want and how to get it, the fire of negative emotions and experiences eventually dies out and the ashes go cold. This is the essence of all emotional healing.

From now on, when something goes wrong for any reason, immediately say, "I am responsible!" and stop the negative emotion from getting started in the first place.

NOW DO THIS

Consider the most negative situation in your life, the one that makes you the most angry whenever you think about it, and cancel the negative emotion by saying firmly to yourself, "I am responsible!"

Then think about all the things you did or didn't do to get yourself into that situation in the first place. As you do, your emotions will calm, you will feel at peace, and often you will find yourself smiling.

This exercise takes tremendous courage and character the first time you try it, but it becomes easier with practice.

6

Change the Water in Your Pond

You have extraordinary mental powers that you seldom use that can bring you all the success and joy you want in life. The truth is that you are where you are and what you are because of the way you *think*, which is largely habitual. When you change the way you think, you change both your inner life and outer life.

The thinking, life, and experiences of many people can be compared to a stagnant pond, where the water never flows out, creating a breeding ground for the kind of creatures that live in brackish water. It is too easy for some people to stop taking in fresh, healthy, positive ideas and messages, rehashing and reliving negative thoughts and becoming generally negative and unmotivated about their lives. But this is not for you.

Changing your thoughts, feelings, beliefs, and attitudes is not easy, but just as you can become physically fit after a long period

Nothing splendid has ever been achieved except by those who dared believe that something inside of them was superior to circumstance.

BRUCE BARTON

of not exercising, you can become positive, happy, and confident—mentally fit—by working on yourself. You can deliberately feed your mind with clean, clear, positive thoughts and images that start to make your life the way you want it.

A Reason for Everything

The Law of Cause and Effect says that every effect, or result, in your life has a specific cause. Nothing happens by accident. Your life today is the result of all your previous thinking and could not be other than it is.

The Law of Sowing and Reaping, which comes from the Bible (Gal. 6:7), says, "Whatsoever a man soweth, that shall he also reap." And the Bible is not an agricultural textbook. It refers to your mind and your personal development. In fact, this law means that whatever you are reaping today, in any area of your life, is the result of what you have sown in the past.

If you want to get a different crop in the future, you have to sow different thoughts in the present. Your outer world is always a reflection of what you are thinking in the moment. "Garbage in, garbage out," as is said in the computer world. But "good in, good out" is also true.

Fortunately, you have complete control over what you think, and by exercising that control, you can turn your frogs into princes and become a completely positive person.

Programming and Preprogramming

Your mind is like an extraordinary computer that you can preprogram to accomplish amazing things. By feeding a steady stream of clean, clear, positive thoughts, wishes, and goals into your mind, preprogram and reprogram yourself to feel and act with confidence and self-control, especially under stress or in times of difficulty.

Perhaps the most important application of the Law of Cause and Effect is "Thoughts are causes, and conditions are effects." This is why you become what you think about most of the time.

What do *you* think about most of the time? Positive, happy people think about what they want and how to get it most of the time. Unhappy, negative people think about what they don't want and who is to blame most of the time. Your goal should be to think about what you want, to program your mind so that you are functioning at your best and feeling terrific about yourself, most of the time.

New Habit Patterns of Thought

There are basically three ways to develop the mental habits of optimism and self-confidence. Fortunately, by the Law of Habit, whatever you repeat over and over eventually becomes a new habit. And you can develop any habit that you find useful and helpful.

Forming a new, positive way of thinking is difficult, but once you have programmed it into your mind, it becomes automatic and easy. This is why Goethe is reported to have said, "Everything is hard before it is easy."

1. The Power of Positive Affirmations

Just as you become what you think about, you become what you talk about, what you say to yourself, most of the time.

But your brain has a negative default setting. If you do not deliberately think positive thoughts about what you want and how to get it, your mind will fill with negative thoughts that will hold you back. With the power of affirmations, your potential is unlimited. When you repeat positive, uplifting words to yourself, they soon begin to take on a power of their own. You begin to think and feel in harmony with your new, positive messages, or programming. Your new positive attitudes cancel out and repel negative thoughts and experiences. You develop a powerful "mental immune system."

The Three Ps of Positive Affirmations Always phrase your affirmations in the three *P*s: personal, present, and positive tense. In the *personal* sense, you precede each mental command with the word "I." You say, for example, "I can do it!" or "I like myself!" or "I earn X number of dollars per year."

In the *present* tense, you state each affirmation as though the event is a current reality and has already happened. "I earn X number of dollars in 2012" or "I weigh X number of pounds." Since your subconscious mind can only accept commands phrased in the present tense, these words are immediately accepted by your subconscious computer and begin working twenty-four hours per day.

The third *P* refers to the *positive* tense. Your subconscious mind cannot process a negative command. You say, "I am a nonsmoker" rather than "I don't smoke anymore." You say, "I am patient and loving" rather than "I don't blow up anymore."

2. You Believe What You See

The second and perhaps most powerful technique of mental programming is *visualization*. The more you feed your mind with clear mental pictures of the person you want to be and the results you want to achieve, the deeper these commands go into your subconscious mind, preprogramming you to think, feel, and act in a certain way when the circumstances require it.

The following are the four keys to powerful and effective visualization for changing your thinking in a positive way:

1. *Vividness:* There is a direct relationship between how clear you make your mental pictures and how rapidly your goals or desired behaviors appear in your life. Creating clear mental pictures, or looking at pictures of what you want, impresses these pictures into your subconscious mind, which then begins attracting people and resources into your life to make your visualization a reality.

2. *Intensity:* The more emotion you can attach to your visualization (and affirmation), the greater impact it has on your thoughts, feelings, and actions. The key is to create the emotion that would accompany the successful realization of your desire. You should consciously "get the feeling" of success and happiness that you would experience when your visualization appears in your life.

3. *Duration:* The longer you can hold your vivid, emotionalized picture in your mind each time, the faster it comes into reality.

4. *Frequency:* The more often you can hold your picture of the ideal goal, life, behavior, or experience that you desire, the faster you program this desire into your subconscious and make it come true.

Rapid Preprogramming Technique You can use a rapid preprogramming technique to mentally prepare yourself for any upcoming event. It requires that you follow four steps in order: verbalize, visualize, emotionalize, and realize.

First, you think about something you want, or the way you want to behave at an upcoming event, and create a personal, present, positive tense command that you then state strongly and clearly, such as "In this upcoming interview or presentation, I am calm, positive, and in complete control."

Second, you create a clear, vivid picture of yourself behaving exactly the way you would be if you were performing at your best.

Third, you emotionalize and "get the feeling" you would have—calm, confident, happy, relaxed—if the situation turned out exactly as you desire.

Finally, you turn this three-part command over to your subconscious mind and allow your subconscious to work on it until the event occurs. You will often be astonished to see the event.or experience happen exactly as you imagined it.

3. Prepare Before the Event

Preprogramming yourself in advance of an important or stressful event will ensure that you are mentally and emotionally prepared to function at the top of your game. This ability to preprogram yourself gives you tremendous control over yourself and how you perform.

If the upcoming event is a few days away, repeat this three-part exercise throughout the day, just as you would practice for an upcoming sports competition. The two best times for this mental rehearsal are just before falling asleep at night and just after waking in the morning, when your subconscious is most receptive to reprogramming.

Affirm your ideal outcome for the event. Visualize the event exactly as you affirm. "Get the feeling" of success and happiness you would enjoy when the event turned out exactly as you desired.

The Power of No

Because of early childhood criticism, most people grow up with fears of rejection. They are afraid of the negative responses of others, even complete strangers whom they have never met.

When you are a child, your favorite word is "yes." May I have some candy? *Yes*. May I have more dessert? *Yes*. May I have a new toy? *Yes*. May I have some money to go to a movie? *Yes*. We love the word "yes," and at the same time, we hate the word "no."

As adults, we are conditioned to seek out "yes" experiences and avoid "no" experiences. But to get ahead, you always have to take a chance that the other person will say *no*. If you avoid the word "no" so often that it becomes a habit, you will short-circuit much of your chance to be successful and happy.

Rejection Is Normal and Natural

Rejection is normal in business and even more so in selling. It is not uncommon for a person to receive five, ten, or even twenty "nos" for every "yes." This is why you must reprogram your mind so that you become completely unafraid of the word "no." When you have no more fear of rejection, your whole future will open up in front of you.

The most powerful word for success is "ask." The more you ask for, the more you will get. This refers to jobs and promotions, dates and relationships, sales, and business opportunities. The future belongs to the askers.

Go for No!

How do you eliminate your fear of being told "no"? By preprogramming yourself to eagerly seek out as many "nos" as possible. You decide that you will have no fear of the word "no" from now on. This discovery changed Brian's life when he was twenty-four, and it changed his son's life when he was twenty-four, as well.

When Brian was twenty-four, he was unskilled and a high school dropout. The only job he could get was straight-commission selling, cold-calling on offices during the day and on homes and apartments during the evening.

On his first day of the job, he was paralyzed with fear. He walked around the block over and over, too afraid to go up to a door and knock. Finally, he pushed himself up to the door, knocked, and waited with his heart pounding.

A nice, little old lady answered, spoke to Brian quite politely, thanked him for calling, and wished him a good day. As he walked down the driveway, Brian made a resolution that he would never be afraid to call on a stranger and ask for an order again.

Face Down the Fear of Rejection

From that day on, he reprogrammed himself to look forward eagerly to rejection, to the word "no." He resolved that from then on, every "no" would spur greater effort and enthusiasm. When he started work in the morning, he could hardly wait to hear the first "no." When he got it, as he inevitably did, he would brighten up and spring into action.

When one of Brian's sons graduated college, he asked his father for advice on what type of job he should get if he wanted to be successful. Brian told him that if he could handle the rejection of cold-calling for one year, he would be psychologically set for life.

He took his father's advice. He got a job cold-calling on homes to sell fiber optic hookups, kept at it for a year, and became a totally different person. His self-confidence went through the roof. He told Brian, "Dad, I know now that I am going to succeed in life because after a year of cold-calling, I'm not afraid of anything!"

You can preprogram yourself to have no fears of rejection or failure by telling yourself over and over that nothing can stop you. Visualize yourself as calm, confident, and smiling. Talk to yourself and create within yourself the emotion that would accompany the success you desire.

By repeating the mental programming techniques of affirmation, visualization, and emotionalization, you take complete control of your mind and emotions, boost your self-confidence, and become a completely positive person.

NOW DO THIS

Think of an upcoming event where you feel apprehensive or fearful about the result or outcome. Create a positive affirmation that states exactly how you would want to perform and how you would want the event to turn out—for example "I am calm, confident, and in complete control in this interview and I get the job (or sale) at the end."

Create a clear, vivid, happy picture of this ideal outcome and play it over and over on the screen of your subconscious mind. You will be amazed at the result the very first time you try it.

7

Look for the Beauty in Frogs

It is not what happens to you in life that determines how you feel; it is how you respond to what happens. It is not the frogs in your life but the way that you deal with those frogs.

Two people may have the same experience, but one will rise above it, let it go, and get on with life. The other person will be crushed, angry, resentful, and unhappy for an extended period of time—same event, two different reactions.

In the book *A Course in Miracles*, Helen Schucman and William Thetford say, "You give meaning to everything you see." This means that nothing contains any emotion, positive or negative, except for the emotion you put into it by the way you think about it.

Difficulties come not to obstruct, but to instruct.

BRIAN TRACY

Make a Decision

The fastest way to transform a negative to a positive and to free yourself from the unhappy experiences of the past is to resolve to see your past in a different way. As soon as you practice the Law of Substitution and exchange a positive thought for a negative thought, your emotions change almost instantly.

Wayne Dyer, the spiritual writer, once said, "It's never too late to have a happy childhood." In other words, by revising your interpretation of the unhappy experiences you had as a child, you can turn them from bad to good, from depressing to elevating, and begin seeing your childhood in a totally new and positive way.

Have a Happy Childhood

Imagine that somewhere on the far side of the universe, long before you were born, you were a *soul* and you were able to search over the earth and select your next parents. Imagine that you chose your parents deliberately so that you could experience the trials and tribulations of a child growing up in that family because that was the only way you could learn, evolve, and grow into a better person.

When you play with this idea and look back at your childhood experiences, you will see your childhood differently. You will begin to identify the lessons you learned from each problem or difficulty you had while you were growing up. By accepting that *you chose your family yourself*, you begin to reinterpret your experiences as positive and educational rather than negative or hurtful.

Think of the impact your parents have had on you. Can you identify how your parents' treatment of you caused the development of your greatest strengths and brought out your best qualities?

Never Complain, Never Explain

Many people spend decades complaining about what their parents did or did not do to or for them when they were growing up. For example, when Brian was in his early thirties and was out on a date with a young woman, over dinner he started to complain about his father and how unkind and critical he had been when Brian was growing up.

The young woman, quite intelligently, listened for a while and then stopped him and asked, "Brian, are you happy to be alive?"

He said, "Of course! I really enjoy my life."

She said, "Well, your father got you here, so stop complaining."

Brian was momentarily stunned, and then he realized that she was right. From that day forward, he has never complained about his father or his childhood again. He realized that if he was happy to be alive, he had no right to criticize the people who brought him into the world.

You can do the same. Whatever your parents did or didn't do, they got you here. They gave you the greatest gift of all—your life. You can always be grateful to them for that.

The Great Power

Imagine out in the universe a great power that loves you and wants the very best for you. This great power wants you to be happy, healthy, and fulfilled. This great power wants you to be successful and prosperous.

This great power also knows that you can rise to greater heights of happiness, joy, and success only by learning certain essential lessons along the way. This power also knows that you have a *perverse* nature: you will not learn unless the lesson hurts.

You cannot learn deeply from reading, watching, or observing the experiences of others. You can learn only when you feel *pain*—physical, emotional, or financial.

A perfect example is the way people approach their health. Most of the time, people continue unthinkingly eating what tastes good and choosing not to exercise. Not until they are struck with some kind of physical ailment or disease do they change their health habits and start eating more nourishing foods and taking better care of their bodies.

The Lessons You Need to Learn

Therefore, to teach you, train you, and guide you toward your higher good, this great power sends you *lessons*, each accompanied by pain, so that you will listen and pay attention.

Napoleon Hill once said, "Every problem or difficulty you face contains the seed of an equal or greater advantage or benefit." Your job is to keep focused on the potential advantage or benefit and keep your mind off the parts of the situation that make you angry or unhappy.

Think of the biggest failures you've experienced in your life. What are the most important lessons you learned from each of them? How have these lessons helped you make better choices and decisions? Especially, what advantages and benefits have come to you as a result of what you learned?

Think About Your Problems Today

Next, think about all the problems that you have in your life right now. Imagine that your problems are like a stack of dinner plates, with your smallest problems on the bottom and your biggest single worry or concern on the top of the stack.

Now, imagine that this major problem contains a gift in the form of a lesson that you need to learn so that you can be happier and more successful in the future. What is that lesson?

One of the most powerful ways to turn negatives into positives, to turn frogs into princes, is to seek the valuable lesson in every problem or difficulty you encounter. If you examine any setback or difficulty, you will always find at least one lesson and sometimes many lessons. As Emmet Fox once wrote, "Great souls learn great lessons from small problems."

You can also use this concept as you approach future challenges or situations that scare you. Trying something new always has an element of fear and anxiety that comes with taking that risk. At one time, Christina was considering being the head of a committee focusing on an issue she felt passionate about. She really wanted to take on the responsibility but was terrified that it would involve public speaking. A good friend told her that she should do it, saying that she would gain rare experiences and develop new skills to use in future endeavors. This advice changed Christina's perspective of fear or potential failure and encouraged her to take on the challenge.

The Lesson You Are Meant to Learn

When you think about your biggest problem today, which probably involves another person, ask yourself, "What is the lesson that I am meant to learn from this problem or difficulty?" Your first answer will likely be simple and superficial. You may say, "Maybe I should do more of this or less of that."

But now comes the most important part. You then ask yourself the key question, "What *else* am I meant to learn in this situation?" This question forces you to drill down *deeper*. This time, the lesson will be more important and significant, if not more painful. Perhaps you need to start doing something different or stop doing something altogether.

Then you ask again, "What *else* is the lesson that I am meant to learn?" You drill even deeper. As you continue asking this question, the lessons will become more and more relevant and painful.

Finally, if you have been wrestling with this major problem for a long time, you will reach the real lesson that you are meant to learn. It is usually that you need to change, get out of, or eliminate this situation altogether.

Many times we find ourselves repeating the same scenario. We have the same issues at work, regardless of the job. We have the same struggles in our relationships, even when the partners change. Not until you dig deep and become aware of these patterns can you really change.

One of the biggest goals in therapy is for people to gain an awareness of these patterns and then figure out what role they are playing in repeating these patterns. For example, we may have had a negative experience when we were younger.

Something about that experience remains unresolved and sticks in our minds. We fail to learn the lesson it contained and subconsciously set up situations to repeat the experience and finally learn the lesson we were supposed to learn.

Control Your Ego

When you finally realize the lesson contained in your unhappy situation, your ego immediately intervenes. As a result, you avoid facing the situation. You practice *denial*, hoping that somehow the situation will get better or go away when, in your heart, you know that it never will.

When you find the courage to face the truth about your situation and take the necessary actions dictated by that truth, something wonderful will happen. All your stress will disappear. You will feel calm and relaxed. You will feel happy and at peace.

When you face the truth—the real lesson you are meant to learn—the problem will be resolved, even before you take the first step.

Change Your Vocabulary

One of the fastest ways to switch your mind from negative to positive whenever something goes wrong is to change your vocabulary. For example, instead of the word "problem," use the word "situation."

"Problem" is *negative*. It immediately conjures up images of loss, delay, and inconvenience. But "situation" is *neutral*. When you say, "We have an interesting situation here," no negative emotional charge is attached to the word. As a result, you remain calm, clear, and more capable of dealing with whatever the situation might be.

An even better word is "challenge." Instead of reacting to a difficulty as if it were a problem or a personal attack on you or your business, instead say, "We have an interesting challenge to deal with here."

A challenge is something that you *rise to*. It brings out the best in you. It is positive and uplifting. We look forward eagerly to challenges because they cause us to stretch and become even better by overcoming them.

The best word of all in describing a problem is "opportunity." Instead of thinking about problems or difficulties, from now on, talk about the unexpected setbacks in your life as challenges or opportunities. An opportunity is something that we all want and look forward to eagerly. When you use this new vocabulary, you will be amazed at how many of your greatest opportunities first appear as problems and difficulties.

Problems Are Inevitable and Unavoidable

No matter how hard you try to avoid them, your life will be an endless series of problems, difficulties, and challenges of all kinds. They come ceaselessly, like the waves of the ocean.

The only interruption in this endless series of problems will be the occasional *crisis*. If you are living an active life, you will probably have a crisis every two to three months. It may be a physical crisis, a financial crisis, a family crisis, or a personal crisis.

By its very nature, a crisis comes "unbidden." It is not an anticipated reversal or setback that you can prepare for. The only question is then, "How do you respond to the crisis: effectively or ineffectively?"

If each person has a crisis of some kind every two or three months, this means that as you read this book, you are in a crisis right *now*, you have just gotten out of a crisis, or you are just about to have a crisis. Your job is to take a deep breath when the crisis occurs, keep calm, look for the good, seek the valuable lesson, and then take action to reduce or minimize the crisis.

Look on the Bright Side

The more you think about what you want and where you are going, the more positive and optimistic you remain. Optimism does not mean that you ignore problems or difficulties, but you choose to approach them positively and constructively.

In changing your thinking, put a positive spin on anything in your life that might make you feel unhappy for any reason. Look for the silver lining to the cloud. As Emerson said, "When it is darkest, men see the stars."

Zero-Based Thinking

Many people suffer from worry and anxiety continually. Often, this behavior is learned from a parent who was also a worrier. Fortunately, as many as 99 percent of the things that you worry about never happen. In fact, the situations that you never thought to worry about are what cause most of your unhappiness.

An effective way to eliminate worry and negative feelings is to practice *zero-based thinking* in every area of your life. Ask yourself, "Is there anything that I am doing in my life that, *knowing what I now know*, I wouldn't start up again today if I had it to do over?"

It takes tremendous courage and character to admit that you made a mistake, that you changed your mind, and that you wouldn't get into this situation again if you had it to do over, based on what you now know.

People hang on to the idea that once they've committed themselves to something, they must see it through at all costs. But as Emerson said, "A foolish consistency is the hobgoblin of little minds." It is a strength, not a weakness, to admit that you did not make the right decision. You should always retain the right to change your mind based on new information.

Once you have determined that you would not get into that situation again, your next question is, "How do I get out, and how fast can I do it?"

As soon as you decide to take action to resolve a difficulty or to get out of a bad situation, your stress disappears. The inaction caused by indecisiveness is what generates most of the stress about the situation. When your course becomes clear, you feel a tremendous sense of relief.

Think Positively and Constructively

You have an extraordinary mind. It can make you happy or sad, depending on the way you use it. As John Milton said in his poem *Paradise Lost*, "The mind is its own place, and in itself can make a heaven of hell, a hell of heaven."

Resolve today to use this wonderful mind of yours to think in a positive and constructive way about who you are, what you want, and where you are going.

From this moment on, refuse to *interpret* situations in a negative way. Instead, look for the good and seek the valuable lesson in every setback and difficulty. Approach each problem as if it were a challenge or an opportunity. Most of all, get so busy working on accomplishing the goals that are important to you that you don't have time for worry or concern.

Seek and You Will Find

The average self-made millionaire in America has been broke or nearly broke two or more times before finally becoming wealthy. But the reason that he became a millionaire was because of the lessons he learned in his earlier mistakes. If he had not failed in business at an earlier age, he would never have developed the knowledge and wisdom necessary to succeed later. His bankruptcy was traumatic at the time, but it contained the seeds of future wealth.

Many people go through a bad marriage or relationship that ends with anger, bitterness, and negative feelings. Later on, they meet the ideal mate, settle down, and are happy for the rest of their lives.

Many happily married people look back at an earlier negative relationship as being essential to their recognizing the good relationship when it came along. They admit that if they had stayed in that bad relationship, they would have been miserable for months or even years.

Suffering and Pain

Humans seem to learn only from *suffering*. Pain is inevitable and unavoidable. But what is really unfortunate is when people experience the pain but fail to identify the lesson that goes with it, which makes it far more likely that they will repeat the mistake that led to the pain.

This is especially true about the way people treat their health. Often people won't invest much time and effort into taking care of themselves until they are diagnosed with an illness or suffer from chronic pain.

Since change is inevitable and unavoidable, whenever you have a reversal of any kind, you can neutralize your feelings toward it by saying, "I see the angel of God in every change," or "Everything happens for a reason." Look upon change as a blessing containing ideas, insights, and advantages that you can use to create an even more wonderful life in the future.

Resistance and Acceptance

Resistance of any kind is a major source of stress, negativity, and even depression. The opposite of resistance is acceptance. It is important for you to *accept* that a change has taken place in your life and then move on.

One of the great rules for success is to accept things that have happened and that you cannot change. Accepting a fact as a reality is the first step to taking charge of yourself and your emotions and then moving on to something higher and better.

The inability to get over a bad situation is a major block that holds people back, often for many years. One of the marks of maturity is to accept that you are not perfect, that you make mistakes. You have made bad choices and decisions in the past that have led to bad results and consequences. So has everyone else.

No Regrets, No Blaming

It is said that a psychiatrist with twenty-five years of experience once told the journalist E. B. White that the most common words he heard at the beginning of a period of emotional counseling were "If only." Telling the stories of their tragedies and long-term unhappiness, his clients said, "If only I had not taken that action, made that decision, accepted that job, invested in that company, or married that person." Unfortunately, regret over mistakes we have made in the past often holds us back from taking advantage of the opportunities of the future.

One of the great secrets of happiness is to eliminate the words "if only" from your vocabulary. Accept that whatever happened has happened and cannot be changed. Perhaps it was unfortunate, but it is over and done with. It is a part of the past. It is a fact. It cannot be changed.

One of the most popular sayings of 2010 was the expression "It is what it is." This should be your motto as well. Accept the situation and move on.

Think About the Future

Inevitably, undesirable changes will take place in your life and work. When they do, accept responsibility, focus on the future, and get busy solving your problems and achieving your goals.

William James of Harvard said, "Be willing to have it so. Acceptance of what has happened is the first step to overcoming the consequences of any misfortune." Remind yourself that you are not a victim. You are a proud, confident, self-reliant person in complete charge of your life and your future. Refuse to wallow in regret or remorse about changes that have happened that you cannot control.

Gain or Loss

The greatest motivation in life is the desire for gain. The second major motivation is the fear of loss. According to psychologists, people fear loss two and a half times more intensely than they desire gain. They may be motivated to a certain degree to achieve a gain, but they are absolutely devastated when they suffer a loss.

If you have a happy relationship, a good job, or a stable financial situation and you lose it for any reason, you can find yourself immersed in grief and regret, often for many months or even years. You need to remember that you were all right before you had what you lost, and you will be all right again in the future without it.

Accept the reality of the situation, whatever it is. Refuse to resist or fight against it. Stop feeling sorry for yourself and telling yourself that "if only" you had done something different, this unfortunate event would not have happened.

Accept the Loss as a Sunk Cost

In accounting, one of the costs that are entered onto a balance sheet is a "sunk cost": an amount of money that has been spent and is now gone forever. It is nonrecoverable, like advertising costs, or purchases of equipment that are now obsolete. You have many sunk costs in your life as well. You will often invest large sums of time, money, and emotion in people, jobs, and investments. But unexpected setbacks and difficulties occur, and your investment turns out to have been wasted.

Instead of throwing good money after bad—investing more time and emotion in a bad relationship or spending more time on something that obviously has no chance of success—you must accept that what you have invested up to now is a sunk cost and resolve to let it go. It is lost forever.

When you develop the strength of character to say, "I was wrong. I made a mistake. I've changed my mind," you will find it much easier to let go of unfortunate events that have occurred and simply accept them as a normal and natural part of your personal growth and development.

 **NOW DO THIS**

Select a problem or challenge you are dealing with in your life today. Look into it for something good that you can gain and a valuable lesson that it contains. Think about the worst possible outcome, resolve to accept it should it occur, and then get busy doing everything possible to make sure that it doesn't happen.

8

Leap Forward Confidently

The pond starts off with cool, clear spring water, ideal for living creatures to grow, swim, and thrive in. Why is it, then, that instead of beautiful, healthy, happy creatures, the negative emotions of *frogs* appear and thrive?

In the same way, each child comes into the world as *pure potential*, with the ability to become an extraordinary person, do wonderful things, and have high levels of health, happiness, and prosperity throughout life. People today can live longer and better than has ever been possible for the human race, and if anything, this situation is getting better year by year.

Children are born complete optimists, fearless and uninhibited, excited, curious, and eager to touch, taste, smell, and feel everything around them. (Have you ever seen a negative baby?)

There is no failure except in no longer trying. There is no defeat except from within, no really insurmountable barrier save our own inherent weakness of purpose.

ORISON SWETT MARDEN

Two Major Pollutants of the Pond

Early in life, however, as the result of mistakes that parents make, children soon begin to experience *destructive criticism* and *lack of love*. These two behaviors, either alone or together, are the primary sources of unhappiness and dysfunction in adult life.

Destructive criticism is the biggest single enemy of human potential. It is worse than cancer or heart disease. While those diseases can ultimately lead to the deterioration and death of an individual, destructive criticism kills the soul of the person but leaves the body walking around.

When parents attempt to control their children by giving love and then taking it away, they create within the child a tremendous insecurity that manifests in self-doubt, anxiety, worry, feelings of inadequacy and undeservingness, demotivation, fear of not living up to others' expectations, striving for perfection, and fear of confrontation or openness.

In combination, *destructive criticism* and *love withheld* weaken the physical and emotional immune system of the child, opening up the child to all kinds of physical and emotional ailments later in life. Physically, the child, and later the adult, can experience fatigue; susceptibility to colds, flu, and stomach ailments; and psychosomatic illnesses.

Weaknesses in the emotional immune system are manifested by susceptibility to a variety of negative emotions, the main sources of unhappiness, frustration, and depression in adult life.

For many years, Christina struggled with chronic stomachaches and headaches. She tried everything to relieve the pain. She changed her diet, took different remedies, and even spent several years in therapy, processing her experiences. Then she discovered something that changed her life. She learned that whenever she did not speak up and tell the truth about something she was thinking or feeling, she would get a headache. Whenever she did not feel right about something and continued to tolerate the situation or remain in an unhealthy relationship, she would get a stomachache.

Ever since she discovered this fact about herself, she's become incredibly aware of listening to her body and remaining as true and authentic as she can be. Now her stomachaches and headaches never persist for more than a couple of minutes and she sees them as reminders. What she learned was that all of us must listen to our bodies and become aware of our emotions. Many people are very sensitive physically when something in their emotional lives is out of balance. The mind and body are intricately connected; the more aware you become of your physical self, the more attuned you become to your emotional needs.

The Fears of Loss and Criticism

There are many negative emotions, but fully 99 percent of them crystallize around the big two: fear of failure and fear of rejection.

Fear of failure is manifested in adult life as a *fear of loss*. People who have been destructively criticized as children fear the loss of money, loss of health, loss of position, loss of security, and loss of the love of other people. No matter how much they achieve in their careers, they are haunted by a fear of having it all taken away and having to start over again with nothing.

The fear of rejection is experienced as a *fear of criticism*. This fear can become so extreme in some individuals that they become hypersensitive to the thoughts, words, opinions, and even the glances of other people, including strangers. In addition, people feel a fear of disapproval, of not being approved of by others whom they are eager to impress. Fear of rejection leads to a fear of the loss of respect of people whose respect is important to them. These people fear embarrassment or ridicule of any kind, especially in the presence of others. The fear of rejection is the root cause of the fear of public speaking, rated ahead of the fear of death among life's major fears.

We often ask two questions in our seminars to help people see the role that fear plays in their lives and decisions:

- *Question 1:* "If you were financially independent today and had all the money that you could ever spend for the rest of your life, what would you do differently? What would you get into or out of? What would you start doing or stop doing?"

  The point is that if you had no fear of poverty, if you had all the money that you wanted or needed, you would probably make dramatic changes in your life.

  People design their lives to compensate for their fears. They accept lower level jobs than they are truly capable of in exchange for security. They stay in relationships where they are unhappy rather than risk being alone.

They choose friends who are passive and indifferent so that they can be sure of never being criticized, embarrassed, or rejected.

- *Question 2:* "What one great thing would you dare to dream if you knew you could not fail?"

  If you were absolutely guaranteed of success in any goal, large or small, long term or short term, what one big, exciting, challenging goal would you set for yourself?

  This question helps people identify the fears that are holding them back. If you were completely guaranteed of success in any one thing that you attempted, you would probably commit to your "heart's desire," the one great, wonderful thing that you were born to do with your life.

The Fully Functioning Person

The psychologist Carl Rogers defines a person who has achieved the higher levels of psychological evolution as a "fully functioning person." This is a person who enjoys high levels of self-esteem and personal contentment and who is completely confident with herself and the world. The most identifiable characteristic of a fully functioning person is that she is completely "nondefensive."

The fully functioning person does not feel that she has to justify or explain herself to other people. She is considerate of the opinions of others, but she lives her life in accordance with her own thoughts, feelings, values, and ideals. She is warm, gracious, happy, and charming and is called a "fully mature, fully integrated personality." She feels that she has nothing to prove to others. To reach this level of personal strength and contentment should be the goal of everyone.

 NOW DO THIS

Imagine that you are rich, successful, powerful, and popular. Create a clear mental picture of yourself as if you had achieved all your goals and you were now financially independent.

How would you feel about yourself if you were already the best person you could imagine yourself becoming? How would you treat other people, your colleagues, coworkers, and staff?

9

Kiss Your Ugly Frogs Good-bye

In talking about what holds you back from becoming everything you are capable of becoming, we must deal with feelings of *guilt and unworthiness*. These feelings can sabotage all your hopes and dreams for success and happiness if you don't learn how to get rid of them.

Feelings of Guilt Are Learned

Children are not born with feelings of guilt. Every guilty feeling that you have as an adult was taught to you by your parents, siblings, and others as you were growing up. And because feelings of guilt have been learned, they can be *unlearned* as well.

Parents usually use guilt on their children because guilt was used on them by their parents, and often by their grandparents, back through the generations. It becomes such a normal part

The power which resides in him is new in nature, and none but he knows what that is which he can do, nor does he know until he has tried.

RALPH WALDO EMERSON

of interacting that people are often unaware that they are using guilt.

Some churches practice "negative religion." In these churches and schools of thought such as socialism and communism, guilt is used systematically and deliberately to undermine emotions, destroy personalities, and make people easily *controllable* by the person using the guilt.

Manipulation and Control

When guilt is practiced deliberately, it is used for two purposes: manipulation and control. Throughout the centuries, people (including parents) have found that if others can be made to feel guilty about something, their emotions can be easily controlled. If their emotions can be controlled, they can be manipulated into doing or not doing something. For this reason, guilt is an insidious and evil emotion used exclusively to destroy people on the inside and lower their resistance to the control of others on the outside.

Children become susceptible to feelings of guilt as the result of destructive criticism and lack of love. In addition, when children are told that they are no good or stupid or a disappointment to their parents or not very competent, they soon begin to develop feelings of unworthiness.

Better or Worse

When children are continually criticized as they are growing up, they soon begin to criticize *themselves*. This self-criticism manifests as negative comparisons with others. All around them they see people who are doing better than they are, whether it is in sports, academics, or social activities. Because they have feelings of inferiority, they conclude naturally that if someone is doing better than they are in some area, that person must be better than them as well.

After negatively comparing themselves with others, guilt-ridden people conclude: "If someone is doing better than I am, that person must be worth *more* than I am. If that person is worth more, then I must be *worthless*."

For this reason, intense feelings of guilt almost inevitably lead to feelings of *worthlessness*. A person who feels worthless, diminished, and of little value becomes insecure, pessimistic, angry, and dissatisfied. Many among the prison population today, for example, have *zero* sense of responsibility or self-esteem. Many of them can clearly remember their fathers or mothers telling them repeatedly that they were no good and they would end up in jail.

Feelings of Victimhood

Feelings of guilt lead very quickly to people seeing themselves as *victims*—of life, circumstances, fate, society, and other factors. This feeling is expressed in the words "I'm not good enough." These individuals continually compare themselves to others and say, "I am not smart enough," "I'm not talented enough," "I'm not competent enough," "I'm no good," "I can't! I can't! I can't!"

 NOW DO THIS

The emotion of guilt often leads to a feeling that you have to take care of someone else's needs or feelings before or instead of your own. You feel you need to seek permission or approval before making a decision. Anticipate a situation that you may be made to feel guilty about and set a boundary in advance.

For example, in the past, Christina would cooperate when her husband committed her to a social event or networking situation that was inconvenient for her. But she resented going just because she felt guilty about putting her own needs first. Now she sets clear boundaries in advance. Her husband must ask her when an engagement comes up and lets her decide if she will attend or not. In this way, they respect each other's space, and guilt cannot influence Christina's behavior.

Avoid Victim Language

Once people develop feelings of guilt, unworthiness, and inferiority, they continue to reinforce those feelings by using *victim language*. Fully 95 percent of the way you think and feel about yourself is determined by the way that you talk to yourself, your inner dialogue, throughout the day. The inner dialogue of guilt-ridden people who see themselves as victims is full of complaining about, criticizing, and blaming others.

In their work and personal relations, they say, "I'll try" or "I'll do my best," which is merely an excuse for failure *in advance*. Whenever people say these words, you know that they are going to fail and disappoint. And they know it too. As Yoda in *Star Wars* said, "*Do* or do not. There is no *try*."

Criticizing and complaining are forms of victim language as well. When you criticize and complain, you position yourself as a victim of those whom you are criticizing and complaining about in the first place.

People who feel like victims continually make *excuses*. They offer up justifications and explanations for not trying, not setting goals, not being punctual, not fulfilling their responsibilities, and not doing the job that they were hired to do. They always see themselves as victims. Nothing is ever their fault.

Free Yourself from Guilt

Here are four steps that you can take to get rid of the feelings of guilt that may have been programmed into you from an early age:

Step one: From this moment on, *never criticize yourself for anything*. Never say anything about yourself that you do not sincerely want to be true. Remember, the most powerful words in your vocabulary are the words that you say to yourself and believe. Make sure that they are positive and upbeat.

The very best words that you can say to yourself, over and over are "I like myself!" "I can do it!" and "I am responsible!" It is not possible to repeat these affirmations and feel negative or guilty at the same time.

Step two: *Refuse to criticize anyone else* for anything. Eliminate destructive criticism from your vocabulary. Be the kind of person from whom "never is heard a discouraging word."

Make it a habit to continually seek out positive things in other people and comment on them. Whenever you say anything nice to another person, for any reason, you raise that person's self-esteem. When you raise the self-esteem of another, your own self-esteem goes up in equal measure.

Step three: *Refuse to use guilt on other people* for any reason. Abolish the use of guilt from your vocabulary, from your family, and from your friendships. Never try to make people feel guilty for something that they have done or not done.

The greatest gift you can give others is that of *unconditional love and acceptance*. This means that you never criticize them for anything that they do or don't do. You praise, approve, or at the very least, remain silent.

Step four: *Refuse to be manipulated by guilt* coming from someone else. From this day forward, reject any attempt to make you feel guilty for any reason.

If your mother or father or someone else tries to make you feel guilty, simply ask, "You're not trying to make me feel guilty, are you?" and remain silent.

Most people won't admit to attempting to manipulate another person using guilt. They will probably say, "Of course not."

But if you ask, "Are you trying to make me feel guilty?" and the other person responds, "Yes, I am," you simply say, "Well, it's *not* going to work."

It is absolutely amazing what happens when you tell people who are accustomed to manipulating you by using guilt that it's not going to work anymore. They may be angry and confused at first. But as they realize that using guilt has no effect on your behavior, they will begin to change and interact with you in a more positive way. Try it and see.

Your great goal in life must be the elimination of negative emotions of all kinds. The two most powerful positive emotion builders are the phrases "I like myself!" and "I am responsible."

The more you like yourself, the more responsibility you will accept. The more responsibility you accept, the more you will like yourself. Each feeds on and reinforces the other.

🐸 NOW DO THIS

Identify one person who manipulates you with guilt and resolve to stop this negative pattern the next time it occurs. You can do this by setting a boundary in advance. For example, if someone doesn't respect your time in a meeting and has a tendency of going over the allotted amount of time, give him a fifteen-minute warning. Tell him that you will have to leave or do something else in fifteen minutes, and then stick to your deadline.

Once you have broken the guilt-throwing syndrome with one person, you will feel confident practicing it with everyone else in your life.

It is human nature to test the boundaries of a situation or relationship and to push as far as you can. The best way to stay strong and protected from the ugly frogs of guilt throwers is to be clear about your boundaries from the beginning. Decide what feels comfortable to you emotionally and physically in your interactions with others. When you have clear boundaries, people may test you but they will eventually accept your limits. When your boundaries are unclear, people will often push the limits and try to get as much from you as they can. Clarity is essential.

 NOW DO THIS

If you can't directly confront someone who makes you feel guilty, try sitting in front of an empty chair and imagine the person were sitting in that chair. Tell her how you feel and say that you won't allow her to make you feel guilty anymore. Tell her that she will now have to assume responsibility for her own life, feelings, and experiences. You are going to take care of yourself and do what makes you happy. If it helps, put a picture of the person on the other chair. If the concept of talking to a chair feels uncomfortable to you, consider practicing this conversation with someone with whom you feel comfortable.

10

Expect the Best
of Your Frog

The primary reason that people are unhappy today is because they are still angry with someone who did or did not do something to them or for them in the past. They still have not forgiven another person for a mistake they feel that person made or a wrong they feel that that person inflicted upon them.

The Developing Personality

When you were a child, your parents took care of everything. They fed you, bathed you, clothed you, took you to school, picked you up, and watched over you. At an early age, most children get the feeling that they are surrounded by the arms of a protector who is all-knowing, all-powerful, and all-wise. As a result, children come to expect that they live in a rational, logical, and orderly universe where their

If you paint in your mind a picture of bright and happy expectations, you put yourself into a position conducive to your goal.

NORMAN VINCENT PEALE

97

all-knowing parents care for them, protect them, and make the best decisions for them.

According to Jean Piaget, the child development specialist who wrote *The Construction of Reality in the Child*, children evolve and mature, moving upward through ever-more-complex levels of understanding of human interaction. At stage four of this development process, early in life, children expect everything to be *fair and just*. If, for any reason, they see or experience what they consider to be injustice in their world, they can become angry or disappointed. They will say, with great emotion, "It's not fair!"

Many negative emotions arise from frustrated expectations, which can occur when events happen *differently* from what a person expected. As a result, the individual lashes out and demands that his expectations be fulfilled. If the situation is not corrected to his liking, he becomes angrier and even more frustrated. It just isn't fair!

Becoming attached to the outcome of a situation is an expectation. We think that determining our desired outcome in advance gives us a sense of control and the ability to plan the future, which is then at least partially unpredictable. The rule is to be clear about what you want but be flexible about the process of achieving it. Try not to expect situations to turn out *exactly* as you want them. Then you won't be disappointed when they turn out in unexpected ways, as they usually do.

Live and Learn

As children grow and mature, they learn that life is not black-or-white but many shades of gray. They experience a series of ups and downs, where sometimes their parents make the right decisions and sometimes they don't.

However, many children *fixate* at a particular level of emotional development, expecting and then demanding that life be fair, just, consistent, and predictable. Once fixated at this level, they can grow up to be adults who demand that life be consistent and predictable. When it is not, they become angry, frustrated, and often depressed.

One of the most important qualities to develop is the ability to tolerate frustration. Many parents are taught to wait and watch as their children figure out how to do something. When parents rush in too soon, not allowing their children an opportunity to feel frustrated and use their own critical thinking to solve the problem, those children can become fixated and never learn to tolerate frustration enough to resolve their own problems. When things don't go as planned, they often become anxious and angry.

The fact is that human beings are *imperfect*. Every individual and every organization consisting of individuals is imperfect. We all make mistakes. We do wicked, senseless, brainless, foolish, and cruel things. This is the way the world is and has always been. To expect otherwise is to court eternal frustration and doubt.

Many people, while growing up, get the idea that the world is supposed to unfold in a particular way. If it does not, instead of adjusting and adapting, they become angry and frustrated and determined to either impose their will on their world or make other people behave in a way more in harmony with what they expect.

The World We Live In

The idea that the world is supposed to be fair and just, the definitions of which are constantly changing and never clear, leads to negative emotions that erupt in personal, political, and social discontent. Many people are perpetually unhappy because they feel that life is not fair and someone is to blame. This leads to the development of two of the worst negative emotions, *envy* and *resentment*, always directed at someone who is perceived to be guilty of something.

Envy and resentment, even though aimed at others, actually arise from deep feelings of inadequacy and inferiority on the part of the person experiencing the emotions. Envy and resentment seem to go around together, arm in arm, like twins. They feed on and reinforce each other.

The Worst of the Seven Deadly Sins

Envy is the only one of the "seven deadly sins" for which there is no payoff for the envious person. Someone can envy another person to the point of being furiously angry inside, or even demonstrating in the streets, but it has no effect on the target, and it gives no benefit or pleasure to the person obsessed with the envy.

A person usually learns envy from a parent or others as the result of being continually told that other people who are more successful or happy are fundamentally bad or dishonest. Alas! This is like saying that some are sick because others are healthy.

In our society, envy drives most social and political policy, both nationally and internationally. Envy is always outwardly directed at others, "the enemy," who are doing better than the person experiencing the feeling of envy. These people are usually called "the rich."

Because, by definition, successful people are bad, they must be brought down or punished in some way. The unfortunate thing about envy is that it can never be satisfied. If anything, envy grows and becomes worse over time. And it causes far more damage to the possessor of the emotion than to the person or group at whom it is aimed.

Admiration Versus Envy

Admiring something that another person has attained or accomplished is not the same as envy. It is good to desire things that other people have because it motivates you to work harder and become better at what you do. Your desire for greater success and accomplishment brings out the best in you. Because of the mental Law of Attraction, one of the best practices you can engage in is to admire the success and accomplishments of others. This sets up a positive force field of energy that attracts into your life opportunities to be successful and accomplished as well.

Because of the mental Law of Repulsion, one of the worst things you can do is to envy or resent others. When you do, you set up a force field of negative energy that drives away and repels success and happiness from your own life. The misunderstanding of this basic concept is a major reason for frustration, failure, and unhappiness in the lives of so many people. By their negative thinking about others, they are actually sabotaging themselves.

Resentment Eats You Up Inside

The twin sister of envy is *resentment*. Resentment also arises when people feel that someone else has achieved or is enjoying better conditions than they are. Certain political philosophies require an *enemy*, someone at whom envy and resentment can be directed to justify the political policies or platform of the party leaders and supporters. Don't allow yourself to be trapped in the emotional quicksand of resentment because of what others say.

The key to eliminating the negative emotions of envy and resentment is to *always want for others what you want for yourself*. If people are doing better than you are in some way, wish them well and admire their success. Think about what you could do to emulate them to achieve the same level of accomplishment. In this way, you set up a force field of positive energy that attracts ideas, people, and resources into your life to achieve the same successes you admire in others.

NOW DO THIS

Identify one or more people whose success you admire and think of something you could learn from them to achieve greater success in your own life. Resolve from now on never to envy or resent those who are more successful than you are.

11

Let Go of Those Painful Frogs

Your goal in life is to be happy, joyous, and emotionally free as much of the time as you possibly can. So you must get rid of all the old baggage and negativity that holds you back, like lead weight, and stops you from achieving all that is possible for you.

Perhaps the most important principle of success and happiness is contained in the Law of Forgiveness, which says that you are mentally healthy to the degree to which you can freely forgive, forget, and let go of any negative experience. This does not mean that you can't learn valuable lessons from unhappy experiences. But you separate the wheat from the chaff. You take the lessons to heart and then let the rest go. John F. Kennedy once said, "Forgive your enemies, but never forget their names."

Each experience through which we pass operates ultimately for our good. This is a correct attitude to adopt and we must ultimately see it in that light.

RAYMOND HOLLIWELL

103

Almost all the great religions teach the importance of forgiveness as the key to inner peace. If you cannot forgive, you are stuck at a lower level of happiness and satisfaction. You are held back year after year by your refusal or unwillingness to let go of a previous hurt.

According to the Law of Substitution, you can deliberately decide to think a thought of forgiveness that frees your mind as a substitute for any thought of anger or hurt that still makes you unhappy.

Two Mechanisms in Your Brain

But here is the kicker: you have both a success mechanism and a failure mechanism in your brain. The success mechanism is activated when you think positive, loving, forgiving thoughts about yourself and other people and focus on your goals. These positive thoughts require conscious, continuous, deliberate effort on your part. They do not happen by accident but by *choice*.

Your failure mechanism, unfortunately, works automatically when you stop thinking about what you want. This means that if you do not *deliberately* choose to think thoughts that make you happy, your mind defaults to negative thoughts that make you unhappy.

Fortunately, by the Law of Habit, if you discipline yourself to keep your mind on positive thoughts, this eventually becomes an automatic way of thinking. When positive thinking becomes a habit, you begin to feel optimistic about yourself and your life.

NOW DO THIS

Carry a small notebook with you for one day. Every time you find yourself thinking a negative thought, stop and instead choose to cancel it with a positive thought, and make a note of your action. Track how often you have to make this choice and note any feelings that come up when you don't feed the negative thought.

Many people automatically feed their negative thoughts as a way to protect themselves from disappointment or possible emotional pain. This is a behavior that has been learned from experience. Fortunately, it can be *unlearned* if you make a conscious effort to change your responses.

The Need to Let Go

As we said before, the primary reason that people are unhappy today is because they have not forgiven another person for a mistake they feel that person made or a wrong they feel that person inflicted upon them.

The decision to practice forgiveness is essential for you to move from being a child to being an adult. When you forgive, you free yourself from negative emotions and guilt, and you free other people as well. You get rid of the baggage of the past and unleash your potential toward the realization of your future.

Forgiveness is the key to joy, happiness, and inner peace. Your ability to freely forgive other people is the mark of how far you have developed as a fully functioning person.

The greatest souls of the ages have been those who have developed themselves to the point where they hold no animosity toward anyone for any reason. Your goal should be the same.

Forgiveness Is Completely Personal

Some people think that forgiving another person is the same as *approving* of his behavior or condoning his unkind or cruel act. They feel that by forgiving, they are actually letting the other person off the hook, letting him go free when it is clear that he did or said something harmful or hurtful.

But here is the key: forgiveness has nothing to do with the other person. Forgiveness has only to do with you. Forgiveness is a perfectly *selfish* act. By forgiving the other person, you do not set him free; you set yourself free.

Your refusal to forgive has no effect on the other person. Your continued anger only makes you feel unhappy and depressed. In fact, if the person you are still angry with knew that you were making yourself miserable thinking angry thoughts about him, he would probably be pleased to hear about it. Is that what you want?

Your Biggest Problems in Life

It is said that 85 percent of our problems in life come from our relationships with other people. Almost all your negative emotions, especially those of anger and guilt, are associated with another person or other persons. When people are asked, "What is the biggest problem, worry, or concern in your life today?" their answers are almost always about other persons—what they have done or what they are doing right now.

Jim Newman used to conduct PACE—Personal and Corporate Effectiveness, a three-day seminar on personal growth and effectiveness. In the seminar, he explained that we all have a series of *green buttons* and *red buttons* on our chests that trigger either happy memories or unhappy memories. By habit, whenever you push a green button, you smile and are happy. Whenever you push a red button, you become angry and want to strike out.

The green buttons are attached to happy memories and associations with people in your life whom you love and enjoy, such as your spouse and children. The red buttons are attached to memories of people who have hurt you, and whom you automatically feel angry about when their names are mentioned.

Rewire Your Buttons by Preprogramming

Jim taught that the key to taking complete control of your emotions is to rewire these buttons by *preprogramming* yourself to think a positive thought rather than a negative thought whenever one of your red buttons is pushed.

Because your emotions operate at such an incredible speed, you can't gain control of them at the moment that they are triggered by a negative memory. You must program them in advance. You do this by saying, "Whenever I think of that person, I will bless, forgive, and let go."

We have discovered that the key to forgiveness is the simple statement "God bless him; I forgive him and wish him well" or "God bless her; I forgive her and wish her well."

It is not possible to be angry at a person while you are praying for him and wishing him well. When you repeat these words over and over, you actually "rewire" your emotions. In almost no time at all, your negative emotions attached to that person stop. Whereas before, the thought or image made you angry, now your response is completely neutral. You feel nothing at all.

From then on, whenever the name or image of that person appears, simply say, "God bless him; I forgive him and I wish him well." When you do, you free yourself to get on with the wonderful life that is possible for you.

The Art of Forgiveness

The art of forgiveness is the key to your future. From now on, when you think of someone who still makes you unhappy, use your wonderful intelligence to think of reasons to forgive and let go. Instead of reminding yourself of the unkind things that person did to hurt you, you instead bless, forgive, and let go. Soon this becomes a habit, and your whole personality changes for the better.

Remember, it takes no intelligence to continually allow yourself to become angry about something that happened in the past and cannot be changed. It takes considerable intelligence and character to bless, forgive, and let go, freeing yourself from the past.

NOW DO THIS

Make a list of three to five people with whom you are still angry and whom you have not forgiven for hurting you in the past. Now, for each person, say to yourself, "I choose to let go of this and I forgive _____ for everything that happened." See how much more positive you feel when you say these words.

Four Sets of People to Forgive

When we talk about forgiveness in our seminars, almost everyone *agrees* that forgiveness is a good policy. They all nod, smile, and say that in the future, they are going to freely forgive others who have hurt them. But when we come to the specific people that they need to forgive, emotional blocks appear.

The four groups of people you must learn to forgive if you truly want to be happy are your parents, your intimate relationships, everyone else, and yourself.

Your Parents

The first people that you have to forgive are your *parents*. Many adults are still angry about something that one of their parents did or did not do to them or for them while they were growing up. They expected that their parents would behave in a particular way, and their parents did something different.

How Long Will You Be Angry?   At a seminar in Orlando, Brian had lunch with Bill, one of the participants. Bill told Brian about his ex-wife, whom he had divorced after more than twenty years of marriage. She had been negative, angry, and complaining the entire time, and he finally decided that he wasn't willing to spend the rest of his life with that kind of a person.

Bill mentioned having lunch with his ex-wife the previous week. He told her that he was concerned about her
negativity and how she seemed to continually criticize other
people and complain about her life and work.

She reacted by saying, "Well, you'd be negative too if
your mother had treated you the way my mother treated
me when I was a teenager."

Bill said, "Susan, you haven't lived with your mother for
more than twenty-five years. How long are you going to use
her as an excuse for your problems as an adult?"

This is an important question for *you* as well. How long
are you going to remain angry about something that happened in the distant past?

Locked in Place   Many people are still locked in place,
still angry at their parents for something that happened
many years ago. Sometimes, people remain angry with their
parents long after their parents have died. As a result, they
remain as children in their own minds. They see themselves
as victims. They feel angry and frustrated and often damage
their relationships with their own spouses and children.

Whether your parents are living or dead, in the same city
or far away, you must freely forgive your parents for everything they did or said that hurt you in any way while you
were growing up. You must say, "God bless them; I forgive
them and wish them well."

They Did Their Best   Your parents did the very best they
could with you based on who they were and what they had.
They gave you all the love they had to give. They had no
more to give than the amount you got.

They were products of their own childhoods and up-bringing. (Their parents were, in turn, products of their upbringing by your great-grandparents.) They could not have done other than what they did. They could not have raised you differently.

Just as you are not perfect, your parents were not perfect either. They had fears and doubts. They made mistakes and did silly, wicked, foolish, cruel, and brainless things. They brought you into the world with the very best intentions and did the best they could with what they knew.

Whenever you are bothered by something your parents did or didn't do, *assume* that if your parents were aware that they had said or done something that caused you pain in any way, they would feel terrible about it. In most cases, they would never have done it intentionally. If you have children yourself, imagine how you would feel if your children told you that you had hurt them in some way. You would probably be surprised. You would never intentionally want to cause pain to your children. Neither did your parents.

Let Them off the Hook   Now you have to forgive them completely for every mistake they ever made in bringing you up. You have to let them off the hook because only in setting your parents free through the practice of forgiveness can you be free yourself. Only by forgiving your parents can you become a fully mature adult.

One of Brian's seminar participants went to his parents' home after the first day of the seminar in which he learned the above principles. At the age of thirty-five, he was still furious about something his father had done to him when he was fifteen years old. This brooding anger was affecting his relationship with his wife and his children. He had to get it off his chest.

His heart was pounding, but he went up to his father and said, "Dad, do you remember what you did when I was fifteen? I just want you to know that I forgive you completely for that, and for every other mistake you ever made in my childhood, and I love you."

His father was a gruff, stern working man. He looked his son in the eye and said in an irritated tone of voice, "I have no idea what you're talking about. I have never done anything in my life that I need to be forgiven for by you."

The son looked at his father with shock. He was stunned. He suddenly realized that he had been angry and upset for twenty years about something his father never even knew that he had done. He shook his head, shook hands with his father, and said good-bye. He walked out into the night feeling as if a huge burden had been lifted off his shoulders.

Write a Letter or Have a Conversation If your relationship with your parents was particularly bad and they are still alive, you may want to write them a letter, spelling out every single thing that you can remember that caused you unhappiness or grief when you were growing up. You can start the letter by saying, "I want to forgive you for the following thing:" At the end of the letter, you can say, "I freely forgive you for everything. I love you and I wish you well." Even if your parents are no longer alive, this exercise can be very helpful.

If you are in contact with your parents, it may also be healing to sit down with them and explore the motivation behind something they said or did to help you alter your perspective of the situation. Often, understanding our parents' thoughts or intentions completely changes the way we feel about an experience. But you must be careful to express curiosity, not accusation, or your parents may feel attacked and become defensive.

Christina encourages her clients to approach their parents by starting the conversation with an explanation of their own experience. For example, "I've been doing some self-exploration and am more aware of a feeling of _____. I remember feeling this way when _____ happened, and I was wondering if you could help me understand what was going on in that situation so I could better understand myself." Make it all about you and not about them.

Christina has a friend who always felt that her parents loved her sister more than her. They treated her sister very differently and seemed to have had a closer relationship with her. Ever since this person was a child, she was aware of a disparity between the way her parents related to her sister and the way they related to her.

She had to work harder for acknowledgment and was not given as many privileges as her sister. As the years went on, she felt more and more hurt, always wondering what was wrong with her and why her parents did not love the two sisters equally. One night she finally decided to confront them and ask why they continued to do certain things for her sister and not for her. What had she done to make them love her less?

They responded with shock and surprise at the thought that they had treated the two children differently. They were absolutely convinced that they treated both children the same and didn't understand Christina's friend's feeling of hurt. She went home that night realizing that her parents would not change or agree about the discrepancy, but she still felt liberated and relieved to have expressed her feelings to her parents. They did not validate her concerns, but they did hear her, and that was all she needed.

Sometimes, just confronting your unhappy feelings and getting them off your chest can liberate you from any anger you may still be feeling.

Once you have forgiven your parents, you will have made a giant stride forward. You will have done something that few people ever do in their entire lives. The very act of forgiving your parents will begin the process of personal liberation. You will start to feel happier and more at peace. You will move mentally and emotionally from a child to an adult.

Intimate Relationships

The second group of people whom you must forgive includes all those in your past *intimate relationships*. Intimate relationships make us very vulnerable to other people. We say and do things in the throes of love and passion that open us up and expose our souls. We give our minds, hearts, and bodies in some of the most intense moments of our lives.

When a romantic relationship falls apart, we are often overwhelmed with many negative emotions. We feel anger and guilt. We experience envy and resentment. We justify and rationalize. We blame, criticize, and condemn. If we don't get our emotions under control, we can experience a mild or even a major form of insanity. We feel as if our emotional lives are plunged into a black hole.

But here again, you must use your wonderful mind to neutralize these negative emotions, to resolve the situation in some way, and to get on with the rest of your life.

What Keeps Them Hanging On   No one can have any control over you unless there is something that you *want* from him or her. In psychology, this is called "unfinished business." We often remain angry and upset over a past relationship because one or more issues have not yet been resolved. One of the worst cases of unfinished business occurs when one person is still in love and wants to rekindle the relationship. But if the other person has moved on emotionally and has no more romantic interest in the past partner, the person who has been left behind emotionally can experience incredibly complicated feelings of anger, guilt, unworthiness, undeservingness, unattractiveness, and inferiority.

The way to practice forgiveness with a past relationship is to accept responsibility for what happened or didn't happen. Instead of blaming the other person, you must accept that you were responsible for getting yourself into the relationship and for keeping yourself in that relationship. You probably knew for some time that it was the wrong relationship to get into or to stay in. You probably knew that you should have gotten out a long time ago.

We recall reading that in a study of several thousand couples who went for marriage counseling prior to the wedding ceremony, one or both parties in fully 38 percent of them admitted privately to the counselor that they did not want to get married to the other person. They felt it was a mistake. But they went through with the marriage anyway because they felt that their families and friends were expecting them to get married.

Please at Least One Person   Here is an important rule: Never do or refrain from doing something because you are worried about what *other people* might think about you. You will eventually learn that nobody was really thinking about you at all. In fact, if you knew how little other people think about you, you would probably be insulted.

You can never be sure that what you do or don't do will please other people, and since marriages and intimate relationships are the most personal interactions you can ever enter into, you should be sure to *please at least yourself* in all cases. Be perfectly selfish. Put your own happiness first. Do only what you feel is the right thing to do for you. Never allow yourself to be influenced by the positive or negative opinions of others.

People Do the Best They Can   Many people will go through a bad marriage and divorce and still be upset and angry ten or twenty years later. They cannot let go of the fact that the marriage, into which they had invested so much, had failed. They cannot forgive the other person for the things that he or she did or didn't do.

But just as with parenting, when people get married, they do the best that they know how. No one enters into a marriage with the intention of making it fail. People always enter into a marriage with the very best hopes, dreams, and aspirations. If later, in the fullness of time, the people change and the marriage doesn't work out, it is not the fault of either party.

No One Is Guilty   In the movie *Good Will Hunting*, the critical point in the relationship between Will Hunting, the patient, and Sean Maguire, the psychologist, comes when Will explains the traumatic experiences of his youth and Sean says to him, "It's not your fault."

This part of the movie is very moving and revealing. Will says, "Yeah, I know that." But Sean repeats, "It's not your fault. It's not your fault. It's not your fault." Finally, Will understands what the psychologist is saying. No matter what happened in his childhood, however traumatic, it was not his fault. At that moment he is free at last.

An unhappy marriage is not your fault either; nor is it the fault of the other person. Two people who were once compatible enough to marry are now no longer compatible. Incompatibility is not a choice. Like the weather, *it just happens*. Two people drift apart and have different thoughts, feelings, and ideas about themselves, their lives, their work, their children, and their place in society. This happens to millions of couples each year. People are constantly growing and evolving, and in relationships we either grow together with common goals and dreams or we grow apart and want different things. It is no one's fault.

Decide to Let It Go   If you are still angry about a relationship or marriage that did not succeed, you must first decide in your own mind to let it go. As long as you cling to the hope that it can somehow be fixed, you can never be free. As long as you insist that the other person accept that he or she is guilty for the breakup, you will never be satisfied. You can never get on with your life. You can never be happy.

Once you have let go of the relationship in your mind, sit down and write "the letter." This is one of the most powerful tools that you will ever use to set yourself free and achieve lasting happiness and fulfillment.

You can write the letter on a piece of paper or as an e-mail. Start by addressing the other person. The opening paragraph is, "It is unfortunate that our marriage did not succeed; however, I accept complete responsibility for my role in the marriage and everything that I did or didn't do that led to its failure."

The middle of the letter is "In addition, I forgive you for everything you did or said that hurt me." At this point, many people make a list of every single thing that they can think of that the other person ever did that still makes them angry when they think about it.

The last line is simply "God bless you. I wish you well."

Now, seal this letter in an envelope, put the correct address and postage on the envelope, and drop it into the nearest mailbox. Or insert the correct e-mail address and press the Send button.

The instant that your hand *lets go* of this letter or you hit Send, and you know that it is irretrievable, you will feel as though an enormous burden has been lifted off of you. You will feel happy and relaxed. You will smile and feel at peace.

In doing this exercise, you must be clear that the point of writing the letter is *personal liberation.* To achieve this, you should express in the letter all your thoughts and feelings regarding the relationship. You then send this letter without any expectation of a response. You are not doing this for a response; you are doing this to let go.

Don't Worry   At this point, people will often ask, "But what if the other person misinterprets the letter and wants to get back together again?"

The answer is simple. Don't worry. You are not writing this letter for the other person. You are writing this letter for *yourself*. You don't care if the other person is happy or unhappy, angry or calm, pleased or displeased.

In many cases, when one person has the courage to accept responsibility and forgive the other person for everything that happened, the other person changes completely. He or she loses all animosity as well, and all the negative emotions drain out of the memory of the relationship. Many couples have said that after one party had written this letter, the two people eventually became good friends and were able to be excellent parents for their children.

Everyone Else

The third group of people you have to forgive is *everyone else* in your life who has ever hurt you in any way. You have to forgive your siblings who may have been unkind to you when you were growing up. You have to forgive your friends of all ages who may have done unkind or cruel things to you. You have to forgive your previous employers who may have treated you unjustly. You have to forgive your business partners and associates who may have cheated you or cost you money. You have to forgive all those with whom you are still angry and whom you still blame for something that they did.

Remember, you are forgiving them for *yourself*. You do not even have to tell them that you have forgiven them. You can simply forgive them in your heart.

Whenever the thought of one of these people comes into your mind, immediately cancel it by blessing him and wishing him well. Refuse to discuss the person or situation with others. This simply heaps fuel on the fire and delays the healing process. Instead, cancel the thought and blot it out of your mind. Eventually, you will think of that person or situation less and less and then not think of him at all.

Yourself

The fourth person you must forgive is *yourself*. Now that you have had the courage and character to forgive everyone in your life who has ever hurt you, you must forgive yourself and let yourself off the hook as well.

Many people are held back because of a mistake they made in years past. Perhaps they did something wicked, brainless, or cruel when they were growing up. Perhaps they hurt someone in an earlier relationship. Perhaps they did something that caused a good deal of pain, cost, and unhappiness to someone in work or business.

If this is true about you, you feel remorse and regret. You feel unhappy and burdened. You wish you had not done or said what you did. You feel guilty and negative. These feelings can hold you back, like weights, from rising to fulfill your complete potential. They can make you feel that you are not deserving of good things in life and can cause you to sabotage your own success.

You Are Not the Same Person   The person you are today and the person who did or said those things in the past are *not* the same person. The person you are today is wiser and more experienced. The person you are today would never do what the person you were in the past did at that time. You cannot continue to punish the person you are today by continually regretting what that other person did a long time ago.

Regret and remorse are not signs of responsibility or conscience. They are actually weaknesses that hold you back. Instead of allowing yourself to "stew in your own juices," say to yourself, "I forgive myself for what I did and I let myself go. That was then and this is now."

Whenever you think of something that you did in the past that you are still unhappy about, forgive yourself and let yourself go.

Set Yourself Free   Many people are miserable and unhappy today because of something that happened or didn't happen years ago. They can't let it go. It may have been a difficult childhood. It could have been a bad marriage. It might have been a lousy job or a poor investment. But whatever it is, because of their inability to forgive and let go, many people are trapped, like dinosaurs in the tar pits, year after year.

If you have led a normal life, you have made all kinds of mistakes and had all kinds of problems with all kinds of people over the years, starting from early childhood. This is normal and natural and part of the human experience. The only question is, "Do you rise above it by practicing forgiveness early and often, or do you let it weigh you down and hold you back?"

One Major Block

Many people will agree that they should forgive all those people who have hurt them in the past. But at the same time, like a card player holding a card close to the chest, they carve out a little area where they *refuse* to forgive. They decide that they will forgive just about everybody they can think of, but *one person* hurt them so much that he or she cannot be allowed to go free.

But holding on to this *single* negative emotion, refusing to forgive this one person or forgive what happened in that situation, is enough to undermine and destroy all your hopes and dreams for health, happiness, and personal fulfillment.

Imagine that you bought a brand-new luxury car, beautifully built and engineered with precision in every detail. There was only one problem. Somehow, during the manufacturing process, a part had been installed incorrectly, causing one front wheel to lock and not rotate when you stepped on the gas. Imagine now that you got into that brand-new car, turned on the ignition, and stepped on the accelerator. What would happen? The car would spin around that front wheel. The back wheels would drive it forward but it would just go in circles, without making any progress.

Here is the point. Even if you have only *one* unconscious block deep in your mind—a negative emotion or memory from an earlier, painful experience—that you cannot forgive, your life will go around in circles indefinitely. No matter how hard you work on the outside, you will not make the kind of progress that you should be making in your family life, parenting, career, health, or financial situation. And the less progress you make, the more dissatisfied you will feel.

In psychotherapy, the patient usually has a single major block hidden deep in the recesses of the mind that manifests itself in feelings of anger, depression, irritation, selfishness, arrogance, insecurity, and undeservingness. The entire process of psychotherapy is to gradually peel away the layers of hurt until the psychotherapist and the patient finally arrive at the one major factor that is blocking progress. Once that factor has been identified and dealt with, the individual will suddenly be free.

NOW DO THIS

Think back about the past and identify the worst possible event that happened to you that could still be causing you to experience feelings of guilt, anger, or unworthiness. Ask yourself, "What were the circumstances?" If you could go back and talk to the person you were in the past, what advice would you give yourself about that situation? What lessons did you learn through that experience that you might not have learned otherwise? Can you find a value or a silver lining to that experience?

Apologize to Others

The final stage of forgiveness requires tremendous *ego strength* and self-confidence. It requires that you apologize to someone whom you have hurt and ask for forgiveness.

Because of the enormous power of justification, identification, judgmentalism, hypersensitivity, and rationalization, the idea of apologizing to another person can be extremely stressful. But if you sincerely desire to be free from something you did in the past that you still feel bad about, you have no choice but to apologize.

Just Do It

Fortunately, this can be a simple process. You can phone the other person right now and say, "Hello, this is _____ , and I just wanted to call you and tell you that I am sorry for what happened, and I hope you will forgive me."

It doesn't matter how the other person responds. He may blow up and become angry. He may hang up the phone. But surprisingly enough, the other person may say, "I am so glad you called. I accept your apology. Why don't we get together for lunch in the near future?"

People who have been estranged for years have gotten back together again and become good friends because one person had the strength of character to say, "I'm sorry."

It may be even better for you to go and see the individual personally, if possible. At the very least, you can sit down and write a letter of apology and mail it or send an e-mail.

Resist the Temptation

Here is a key point with regard to apologizing: resist the temptation to tell your side of the story, to defend yourself, or to justify your past behavior. Just accept responsibility and say, "I'm sorry" and leave it at that. If you start to justify and rationalize your behavior, you are in danger of "taking it back," and undermining the whole purpose of the apology, which is to set yourself free.

Finally, if you feel that it is necessary and correct, offer to compensate or make restitution of some kind. Be generous.

Remember, in life you will make many mistakes, but *you can never be too kind or too fair.*

Your ability to forgive yourself and others early and often and to refuse to hold a grudge or feel negative toward others will put you on the side of the angels. Forgiveness will set you free, liberate your energies, and make you a completely positive person. Try it and see.

NOW DO THIS

Select one person from your past who still triggers anger and negative emotions whenever you think about him or her. Select the very worst negative memory that you still have.

Use this person and this feeling of anger and blame as your test case. From this moment forward, begin forgiving this person every time you think of him or her. Accept that you were partially responsible for what happened. Keep blessing, forgiving, and wishing the person well until all the anger and negativity dissolve and drift away.

Then, make a list of every other person in your life with whom you are still angry. Go down the list and forgive each person until you are completely calm, relaxed, and at peace.

12

Seven Keys to a Positive Personality

Your *physical diet* has a large impact on your levels of health and energy. If you eat fresh, healthy, high-quality foods of all kinds and avoid the foods that are bad for you, you will have more energy, be generally resistant to most diseases, sleep better, and feel healthier and happier.

In the same way, your *mental diet* largely determines your character and your personality and almost everything that happens to you in life. When you feed your mind with positive ideas, information, books, conversations, audio programs, and thoughts, you develop a more positive and effective personality. You become more influential and persuasive. You enjoy greater self-confidence and self-esteem.

Those who work with computers use the expression "GIGO," or "garbage in, garbage out." But the reverse is also true, "Good in, good out."

Help people become more motivated by guiding them to the source of their own power.

PAUL G. THOMAS

When you make a clear, unequivocal decision that you are going to take complete control over your mind, eliminate the negative emotions and thoughts that may have held you back in the past, and become a completely positive person, you can actually bring about your own personal transformation.

Be the Best You Can Be

Mental fitness is like physical fitness. You develop high levels of self-esteem and a positive mental attitude with training and practice. Here are the seven keys to becoming a completely positive person:

1. *Positive self-talk:* Speak to yourself positively; control your inner dialog. Use affirmations phrased in the positive, present, and personal tense: "I like myself!" "I can do it!" "I feel terrific!" "I am responsible!"

   We believe that fully 95 percent of your emotions are determined by the way you talk to yourself as you go throughout your day. The sad fact is that if you do not deliberately and consciously talk to yourself in a positive and constructive way, you will, by default, think about things that will make you unhappy or cause you worry and anxiety.

   As we said before, your mind is like a garden. If you do not deliberately plant flowers and tend them carefully, weeds will grow without any encouragement at all.

2. *Positive visualization:* Perhaps the most powerful ability that you have is the ability to visualize and see your goals as already accomplished.

   Create a clear, exciting picture of your goal and your ideal life, and replay this picture in your mind over and over. All improvement in your life begins with an improvement in your mental pictures. As you "see" yourself on the inside, you will "be" on the outside.

3. *Positive people:* Your choice of the people with whom you live, work, and associate will have more of an impact on your emotions and your success than any other factor. Decide today to associate with winners, with positive people, with people who are happy and optimistic and who are going somewhere with their lives.

   Avoid negative people at all costs. Negative people are the primary source of most of life's unhappiness. Resolve that from today onward, you are not going to have stressful or negative people in your life.

4. *Positive mental food:* Just as your body is healthy to the degree to which you eat healthy, nutritious foods, your mind is healthy to the degree to which you feed it with "mental protein" rather than "mental candy."

   Read books, magazines, and articles that are educational, inspirational, or motivational. Feed your mind with information and ideas that are uplifting and that make you feel happy and more confident about yourself and your world.

Listen to positive, constructive CDs and audio programs in your car and on your MP3 player or iPod.
Feed your mind continually with positive messages
that help you think and act better and make you more
capable and competent in your field.

Watch positive and educational DVDs, educational
television programs, online courses, and other uplifting material that increases your knowledge and makes
you feel good about yourself and your life.

5. *Positive training and development:* Almost everyone in
our society starts off with limited resources, sometimes
with no money at all. Virtually all fortunes begin with
the sale of personal services of some kind. All the people who are at the top today were once at the bottom,
and sometimes they fell to the bottom several times.

The miracle of lifelong learning and personal improvement is what takes you from rags to riches, from
poverty to affluence, and from underachievement to
success and financial independence. As Jim Rohn
said, "Formal education will make you a living; self-
education will make you a fortune."

When you dedicate yourself to learning and growing and becoming better and more effective in your
thoughts and actions, you take complete control of
your life and dramatically increase the speed at which
you move upward to greater heights.

6. *Positive health habits:* Take excellent care of your physical health. Resolve today that you are going to live to

be eighty, ninety, or one hundred years old and still be dancing in the evenings.

Eat excellent foods, healthy and nutritious, and eat them sparingly and in proper balance. An excellent diet will have an immediate, positive effect on your thoughts and feelings.

Resolve to get regular exercise, at least two hundred minutes of motion per week, walking, running, swimming, bicycling, or working out on equipment in the gym. When you exercise on a regular basis, you feel happier and healthier and experience lower levels of stress and fatigue than a person who sits on the couch and watches television all evening.

Especially, get ample rest and relaxation. You need to recharge your batteries on a regular basis, especially when you are going through periods of stress or difficulty. Vince Lombardi once said, "Fatigue makes cowards of us all."

Some of the factors that predispose us to negative emotions of all kinds are poor health habits, fatigue, lack of exercise, and nonstop work. Seek balance in your life.

7. *Positive expectations:* Having positive expectations is one of the most powerful techniques you can use to become a positive person and to ensure positive outcomes and better results in your life.

Your expectations become your own self-fulfilling prophesies. Whatever you expect, with confidence, seems to come into your life.

Since you can control your expectations, you should always expect the best. Expect to be successful. Expect to be popular when you meet new people. Expect to achieve great goals and create a wonderful life for yourself. When you constantly expect good things to happen, you will seldom be disappointed.

CONCLUSION

Action
Is Everything

Action is everything! Resolve today to put these ideas to work, to kiss your frogs, to face the unpleasant situations in your life, and to become a completely positive, happy, healthy person.

♔ Identify the frogs in your life, the negative people, situations, and memories that keep you stuck in the swamp of negative emotions.

♔ Realize and accept that you are a thoroughly good person with enormous potential to live an extraordinary life.

♔ Decide today to confront any negative situation in your life and get rid of it once and for all.

♔ Identify the factors that cause you to experience negative emotions, especially anger, and begin changing your thinking in each area. Repeat the words "I am responsible" over and over until they become a permanent part of your personality.

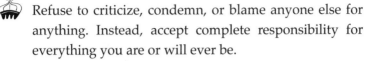 Refuse to criticize, condemn, or blame anyone else for anything. Instead, accept complete responsibility for everything you are or will ever be.

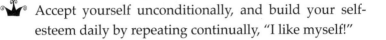 Accept yourself unconditionally, and build your self-esteem daily by repeating continually, "I like myself!"

 Decide exactly what you really want in life and then think and talk about it all the time. Get so busy working on achieving something that is important to you that you have no time to think about the frogs that can hold you back.

Free yourself from the feelings of guilt by refusing to be manipulated by the frog of guilt and by refusing to use it on anyone else.

Look for something good in every problem, difficulty, or frog you face. You will always find some way to benefit.

Seek the valuable lesson in every setback or obstacle, and strive to learn from every problem you face, every frog you have to deal with.

Treat every person you meet as if he or she was the most important person in the world, the handsome prince or the beautiful princess.

Practice the seven keys to becoming a purely positive person and release your full potential to become everything you are capable of becoming.

You are a thoroughly good person. You are designed for success and engineered for greatness. You have within you more talent and ability than you could use in one hundred lifetimes. There is virtually nothing that you can't accomplish if you want it long enough and hard enough and are willing to work for it.

When you learn to release your mental brakes, forgive everyone who has ever hurt you in any way, and dedicate yourself to becoming an excellent person in your relationships with others and in your work, you take full control of your destiny. You maximize all your abilities and put yourself onto the high road of health, happiness, loving relationships, maximum achievement, and complete fulfillment.

ACKNOWLEDGMENTS

We would both like to thank the incredible people at Berrett-Koehler, especially Steve Piersanti, publisher and editor, who guided and shaped this book from the original idea to the finished book, Jeevan Sivasubramaniam, for his insightful and helpful comments and additions, our initial reviewers—Chloe Park, Julie Pinkerton, Adryan Russ, Chris Morris, and Brita Adkinson—whose ideas and suggestions were invaluable in shaping and improving the manuscript, and all the fine people at Berrett-Koehler whose ideas and inspirations went into this final version.

I, Brian, would like to thank the millions of my students in fifty-eight countries who have embraced these ideas and used them to get rid of the negative beliefs and emotions holding them back from becoming the extraordinary people they were meant to be.

Most of all, I thank my wonderful wife, Barbara, who has worked with me since we began teaching these ideas in seminars and workshops in 1981 and whose knowledge of psychology and personality development contributed immeasurably to the polishing of the presentation and delivery of these ideas and concepts, making them acceptable and assimilable to people worldwide.

I, Christina, would like to acknowledge several people who have encouraged, challenged, and loved me. First are the members of my family: Mom, Dad, Michael, Tasha, David, Sara, and Cat. Second are the members of my other family: Jackie, Larry, Scott, GG, Mr. GG, and Danielle, who is the best older sister I could hope for.

I also want to thank my dear friends Niki Rein and Mina Neuberg, who see my potential and continue to love and encourage me to be the best I can be. Thank you to my mentors, who all in their own individual ways have taught me to question, explore, trust, and embrace so many wonderful principles in human development and psychology. Thanks also to Debbie Couillard, Larry Knabb, Judy Grear, Gerald Jellison, Debbie Brunsten, Astrid Shwartz, and Paul Chek, and to Josie Kelly, who has guided me through the swamp and taught me how to embrace my own frogs. Of course, a special thanks to my dad, Brian, and my mother, Barbara, who through their wisdom have raised me to be a confident, strong-willed, and persistent woman. Thank you so much for having faith in my knowledge and ability. I'm thrilled to have been a coauthor on this book.

SERVICES OFFERED

Brian Tracy
SPEAKER, CONSULTANT, EXECUTIVE COACH

Brian Tracy is one of the top professional speakers in the world, addressing more than 250,000 people each year throughout the United States, Europe, Asia, and Australia. His keynote speeches, talks, and seminars are described as "inspiring, entertaining, informative, and motivational." His audiences include businesses and associations of every size and type, including many Fortune 500 companies. Since he began speaking professionally, Brian has shared his ideas with more than five million people in fifty-eight countries and has served as a consultant and trainer for more than one thousand corporations. Some of his topics include the following:

21st Century Thinking
How to outthink, outperform, outsell, and outstrategize your competition to get superior results in a turbulent, fast-changing business environment.

Leadership in the New Millennium
How to apply the most powerful leadership principles ever discovered to manage, motivate, and get better results, faster than ever before.

Advanced Selling Strategies
How to outthink, outperform, and outsell your competition using the most advanced strategies and tactics known to modern selling.

The Power of Personal Productivity
How to get organized, set clear priorities, focus on key tasks, overcome procrastination, concentrate single-mindedly on your most important tasks, and get more done in a day than many people get done in a week. You learn the strategies and techniques of the most productive people in every field.

For full information on booking Brian to speak at your next meeting or conference, visit Brian Tracy International at www.briantracy.com, or call 858-436-7300 for a free promotional package. Brian will carefully customize his talk for you and for your needs.

Build a Great Business!
Brian Tracy's Total Business Mastery Seminar
(Two-Day Live Seminar/Workshop)

In this two-and-a-half-day Total Business Mastery Seminar, Brian Tracy gives you a practical and immediately actionable, street-smart MBA. You learn the ten most powerful and important principles for business success, which you can put to work the next day.

Throughout this two-day program, you will work through an action guide and eye-opening exercises that enable you to apply every idea to your own business, sometimes before the seminar is over. You'll work on your business and mastermind with your peers about your strengths, weaknesses, challenges, and greatest opportunities. You'll leave this seminar with a written plan to increase your sales, reduce your costs, and boost your profits.

You learn how to become a more effective executive and generate the critical numbers essential for business success.

You learn and internalize the ten great areas of business success, becoming one of the best businesspeople in your industry.

This entire program can be presented, with all materials, to individuals, corporations, and organizations of almost any size.

**For more information go to www.briantracy.com/tbm
or call (858) 436-7300**

*Learn the practical, proven skills and techniques
that you need to survive, thrive, and grow
in any business and in any market.*

Christina Tracy Stein
PSYCHOTHERAPIST, PERFORMANCE COACH, FACILITATOR

Christina Tracy Stein offers the following services:

Psychotherapy
As a therapist, Christina believes the most significant aspect of working together is the relationship. She comes from a place of unconditional positive regard and believes that not only are you deserving of living an authentic life, but you are capable of discovering what your truth may be and aligning with it to fulfill your potential.

Christina strongly believes that therapy is a collaboration, and her goal as your therapist is to help you become more self-actualized so that you feel empowered in your life and are able to

- Create more fulfilling relationships
- Develop better ways to handle stress and anxiety
- Work through issues that are causing you to feel depressed
- Achieve a greater sense of enjoyment, satisfaction, and meaning in your life
- Overcome addictive behaviors and self-destructive habits
- Improve your self-esteem and self-confidence
- Learn to love and appreciate yourself
- Become re-engaged with your life
- Challenge your self-defeating thoughts
- Develop healthy coping strategies
- Understand negative patterns

Personal Performance Coaching
Christina offers a free initial consultation where potential clients fill out a short questionnaire and then spend twenty to thirty minutes discussing the process and deciding if coaching is right for them. Christina uses the DISC Assessment initially to gain an understanding of how you think and feel. With better knowledge of your personality, she then works with you to examine all aspects of your life. On that foundation, you then set clear goals. Together you work toward the goals that enable you to be happier, more effective, and more successful.

Healthy Sexuality Consultations and Workshops
In her work, Christina puts a lot of emphasis on sexuality and
desire. She strongly believes that healthy sexuality is an essential part of a person's ability to connect with his or her creative
energy and experience greater vitality. Christina feels that discovering or reconnecting with your unique erotic nature allows
you to feel alive and engaged in the world, as well as gain a
strong sense of personal power.

Christina conducts bimonthly workshops in her private practice and is hired by private organizations to facilitate workshops
with their clientele. She often encourages her workshop participants to seek out a private consultation with her after attending
her workshop. This continued exploration reinforces the new
awareness and connection with one's sexuality. She is available for
phone consultations.

**For more information on therapy, coaching,
or workshops, go to www.christinatracystein.com
or call (310) 712-5441**

ABOUT THE AUTHORS

 **Brian Tracy** is a professional speaker, trainer, seminar leader, and consultant and is the chairman of Brian Tracy International, a training and consulting company based in Solana Beach, California.

Brian learned his lessons the hard way. He left high school without graduating and worked as a laborer for several years. In his midtwenties he became a salesman and began his climb up the business ladder. Year by year, studying and applying every idea, method, and technique he could find, he worked his way up to become chief operating officer of a $276 million development company.

In 1981 he began teaching his success principles in talks and seminars around the country. Today, his books, audio programs, and video seminars have been translated into thirty-eight languages and are used in fifty-eight countries.

He is the bestselling author of more than fifty books, including *Eat That Frog!*, *Goals!*, *Maximum Achievement*, *Advanced Selling Strategies*, *Focal Point*, and *The 100 Absolutely*

Unbreakable Laws of Business Success. He has written and produced more than five hundred audio and video learning programs that are used worldwide.

Brian is happily married and has four children. He is active in community affairs and lives in Solana Beach, California.

Christina Tracy Stein graduated with a bachelor of arts in psychology from the University of Southern California, received her master's degree in clinical psychology from Antioch University, has a Marriage and Family Therapist license from the California Board of Behavioral Sciences, is a member of both the American Association for Marriage and Family Therapy and the California Association of Marriage and Family Therapy, and is a Certified Nutrition and Lifestyle Coach.

Prior to beginning her private practice, Christina worked at the Maple Counseling Center, Beverly Hills, California, where she participated in the Intake and Assessment, Adult Counseling, and Group Programs. She has spent more than five thousand hours with individuals, couples, and groups doing assessments, psychotherapy, and personal counseling.

With her passion for facilitating personal growth and awareness, Christina focuses on helping individuals discover their strengths and accomplish their goals, leading to a more inspiring life.

As a personal development coach, Christina works with individuals to examine all aspects of their lives and set clear goals that enable them to be more effective and successful. She directs and facilitates growth by providing insights as well as practical information and access to resources that benefit each individual.

Christina feels that individuals are capable of discovering their truth, and by aligning with that truth, they will fulfill their potential. She works collaboratively with her clients as a therapist, coach, and facilitator.

Christina has a private practice in Santa Monica, California. She is married and has three children.

Also by Brian Tracy

Flight Plan
The Real Secret of Success

Life is a journey, and as with any other journey you need clear goals, plans, and schedules to get from where you are now to where you want to be—a flight plan. In this powerful, practical book, Brian Tracy uses the metaphor of an airplane trip to help you chart a course to greater achievement, happiness, and personal fulfillment.

Hardcover, 168 pages, ISBN 978-1-57675-497-9
Paperback, ISBN 978-1-60509-275-1
PDF ebook, ISBN 978-1-57675-556-3

The 100 Absolutely Unbreakable Laws of Business Success

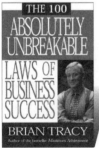

Why are some people more successful in business than others? Why do some businesses flourish where others fail? In this eye-opening practical guide, Brian Tracy presents a set of universal laws that lie behind the success of businesspeople everywhere. He provides numerous real-life examples to illustrate how each law functions and practical guidance and exercises for applying each to your life and work.

Paperback, 336 pages, ISBN 978-1-57675-126-8
PDF ebook, ISBN 978-1-57675-794-9

BK Berrett–Koehler Publishers, Inc.
San Francisco, *www.bkconnection.com*

800.929.2929

Also by Brian Tracy

Be a Sales Superstar

21 Great Ways to Sell More, Faster, Easier in Tough Markets

Based on his close work with top salespeople and his keen observation of their methods, as well as his own experiences as a record-breaking salesman, Brian Tracy presents key ideas and techniques that address both the *inner* game of selling (the mental component) and the *outer* game of selling (the methods and techniques of actually making the sale).

Paperback, 168 pages, ISBN 978-1-57675-273-9
PDF ebook, ISBN 978-1-60509-836-4

The 21 Success Secrets of Self-Made Millionaires

How to Achieve Financial Independence Faster and Easier Than You Ever Thought Possible

Brian Tracy shows how anyone, no matter where he or she is in life at this moment, can become a millionaire. The advice in this book is based on Tracy's decades of careful analysis of the habits and practices of hundreds of self-made millionaires, as well as his own rags-to-riches experience. A net worth of $1,000,000? Why not you?

Hardcover, 96 pages, ISBN 978-1-58376-205-9
PDF ebook, ISBN 978-1-57675-918-9

BK® Berrett–Koehler Publishers, Inc.
San Francisco, *www.bkconnection.com*

800.929.2929

Also by Brian Tracy

Get Paid More and Promoted Faster

21 Great Ways to Get Ahead in Your Career

Brian Tracy reveals how you can apply the secrets and strategies used by the highest-paid people in our society to maximize your own strengths, make yourself more valuable, and become virtually indispensable to your company. This book will help you develop the discipline and determination you need to get more done, earn the respect of coworkers and bosses, and move upward to greater and greater levels of success.

Hardcover, 128 pages, ISBN 978-1-58376-207-3
PDF ebook, ISBN 978-1-57675-802-1

Hire and Keep the Best People

21 Practical and Proven Techniques You Can Use Immediately

From corner cubicle to corporate suite, managers today say their biggest concern is the competition for talent, yet most managers have never received any formal training in the process of personnel selection. In a single brief volume, Brian Tracy draws on decades of training managers in the art of employee selection to pinpoint the twenty-one most important, proven principles of employee recruitment and retention.

Hardcover, 144 pages, ISBN 978-1-57675-169-5
PDF ebook, ISBN 978-1-60994-186-4

BK® Berrett–Koehler Publishers, Inc.
San Francisco, *www.bkconnection.com*   **800.929.2929**

Berrett–Koehler
Publishers

Berrett-Koehler is an independent publisher dedicated to an ambitious mission: *Creating a World That Works for All*.

We believe that to truly create a better world, action is needed at all levels—individual, organizational, and societal. At the individual level, our publications help people align their lives with their values and with their aspirations for a better world. At the organizational level, our publications promote progressive leadership and management practices, socially responsible approaches to business, and humane and effective organizations. At the societal level, our publications advance social and economic justice, shared prosperity, sustainability, and new solutions to national and global issues.

A major theme of our publications is "Opening Up New Space." Berrett-Koehler titles challenge conventional thinking, introduce new ideas, and foster positive change. Their common quest is changing the underlying beliefs, mindsets, institutions, and structures that keep generating the same cycles of problems, no matter who our leaders are or what improvement programs we adopt.

We strive to practice what we preach—to operate our publishing company in line with the ideas in our books. At the core of our approach is stewardship, which we define as a deep sense of responsibility to administer the company for the benefit of all of our "stakeholder" groups: authors, customers, employees, investors, service providers, and the communities and environment around us.

We are grateful to the thousands of readers, authors, and other friends of the company who consider themselves to be part of the "BK Community." We hope that you, too, will join us in our mission.

A BK Life Book

This book is part of our BK Life series. BK Life books change people's lives. They help individuals improve their lives in ways that are beneficial for the families, organizations, communities, nations, and world in which they live and work. To find out more, visit **www.bk-life.com**.

Berrett–Koehler
Publishers

A community dedicated to creating
a world that works for all

Visit Our Website: www.bkconnection.com

Read book excerpts, see author videos and Internet movies, read our authors' blogs, join discussion groups, download book apps, find out about the BK Affiliate Network, browse subject-area libraries of books, get special discounts, and more!

Subscribe to Our Free E-Newsletter, the *BK Communiqué*

Be the first to hear about new publications, special discount offers, exclusive articles, news about bestsellers, and more! Get on the list for our free e-newsletter by going to **www.bkconnection.com**.

Get Quantity Discounts

Berrett-Koehler books are available at quantity discounts for orders of ten or more copies. Please call us toll-free at (800) 929-2929 or email us at bkp.orders@aidcvt.com.

Join the BK Community

BKcommunity.com is a virtual meeting place where people from around the world can engage with kindred spirits to create a world that works for all. BKcommunity.com members may create their own profiles, blog, start and participate in forums and discussion groups, post photos and videos, answer surveys, announce and register for upcoming events, and chat with others online in real time. Please join the conversation!